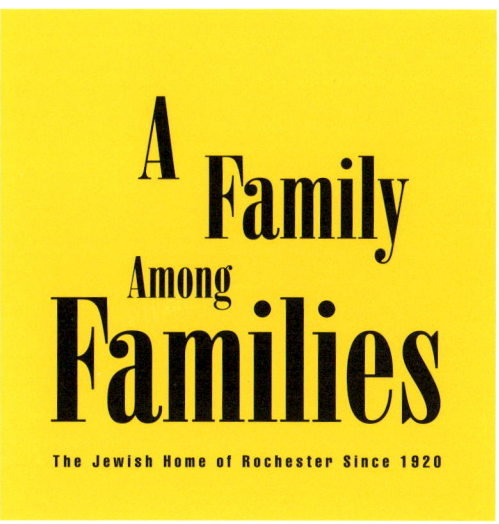

A Family
Among
Families

The Jewish Home of Rochester Since 1920

Honor your

father and your mother

so that your days will

be lengthened...

Exodus   20:12

A Family Among Families

The Jewish Home of Rochester Since 1920

Written by

Michael Dobkowski
and Barbara I. Lovenheim

Research by

Catherine Samson

Design by

Kathleen M. Mannix

A Gift of

Adelaide and Robert Weinberg

Published by

Jewish Home Foundation, Inc.

1 9 9 8

Library of Congress Catalog Card Number: 97-73986

ISBN 09651374-1-4

Printed by The Stinehour Press, Lunenburg, Vermont

Published by Jewish Home Foundation, Inc., Rochester, New York

Contents

Adelaide and Robert Weinberg

The Jewish Home of Rochester has touched the lives of so many in this community. We have fond and wonderful memories of the early days on St. Paul Street and frankly stand in awe at what has been accomplished to this point. Many members of our families and countless friends have been involved in making the Home the community resource it has become. Adelaide and I have contributed our small part as well. We have seen it as a privilege and as a labor of love.

This book really began when Linda Rubens, then director of development of the Jewish Home Foundation, asked me to serve on the Archives Committee. I thank her for that opportunity. At our first meeting, the group was taken into a storage room, where we found stacks of memorabilia consisting of thousands of photographs, newspaper articles, slides, papers and other materials pertinent to the Home—all to be categorized and eventually computerized.

I thought such a process to be insurmountable, but if Albert Einstein could devise the theory of relativity, every problem had a solution. We found our solution with the capable assistance of Catherine Samson, a professional whom we engaged to help organize our archives and to contribute to the publication of this book.

At the second meeting of our group, I suggested that the Home mark its 75th anniversary by publishing a history. Let us tell the world of this miracle that, from a very humble beginning, developed into a facility that today is one of the best in the country. The purpose of this book is to give the community knowledge of the remarkable story of this institution. In many respects, the Home's success is a mirror image of the success and the values of the Rochester Jewish community itself. How we care for the elderly and those in need is really a barometer of our "health" as a community. We have done extremely well, and this book documents that story. It also gives due recognition to the leaders, volunteers, administrators and staff who have been responsible for the Home. And it honors many of the individuals who have given so much of their time, resources and talents to make all of these remarkable achievements possible.

The book records such achievements for present and future generations so that they can learn of these accomplishments and build upon them. We hope and expect that our children and grandchildren will be moved by the work of their elders and will receive inspiration to do the same. The standards already achieved must go forth and never be lowered. If The Summit at Brighton Retirement Community is any indication, we are well on our way.

Finally, this book, which records the history of the Home, does so with a view to the future. If we don't know and appreciate the past, we will never be able to embrace the future with confidence. We hope this book will help provide that context to bridge the past and the future. May the Almighty look favorably upon this enterprise, the enterprise of caring for the elderly and infirm inspired by our Jewish values; guide and bless it, and give inspiration, strength and comfort to everyone who is committed to its success.

Adelaide and Bob Weinberg

Eli Rudin (left), Will Greenberg (right), Arnold Gissin (standing)

The history of the Jewish community of Rochester passes through the Jewish Home. So many lives in this city have been touched by this remarkable community resource. *A Family Among Families* captures the essence of a nearly eighty-year history, a story filled with dedicated and courageous people who have devoted themselves to the care of the Jewish elderly in this community. It is also a story about continuity and connection, about several generations of leaders and activists who have followed in the footsteps of grandparents and parents to continue their legacy.

This book evolved out of the effort to collect and preserve documentary material related to the history of the Home. A group of individuals headed by the retired director of physical therapy, Judy Lurie, and former executive director Will Greenberg, established an archives committee and began to survey eighty years of our history, which they found in the form of documents, photographs, testimonials and newsletters. Bob Weinberg, a member of this committee, "assayed" these precious nuggets and understood that they contained a story that should be told. He helped reshape these many nuggets and encouraged those working with them by his generous support to fashion the material into this wonderful book.

As the former and current Jewish Home administrators who make their homes in the Rochester Jewish community, it is our collective pleasure, pride and delight to introduce to our community this chronicle of a caring tradition. This is a tradition begun by a group of women in the 1920s who set the foundation for subsequent generations to follow. It has been our pleasure to add, each in our own styles, to what was given to us, and we hope that our contributions will be as useful to future leadership as were those left for us.

We congratulate and thank all involved with the Home, those who came before us, those who worked with us and those leaders, activists and volunteers who are yet to emerge. This is really their history. Many individuals are mentioned in the book. Not everyone, however, could be so recognized. We apologize for any omissions and express our deepest gratitude to all who have given of their time and resources to the Home. What stands today, a source of much pride, would not have been possible without their selfless efforts. We especially thank Arky and Bob Weinberg for their generosity in underwriting this special gift to our Jewish Home family.

Eli Rudin, Will Greenberg, and Arnold Gissin

This oil painting, Rabbi 1892, by J. Tepper is part of the extensive Jewish Home of Rochester art collection. The painting was on display at the original Home.

Beginning a Community

The Jewish Home of Rochester, a handsome six-story brick-and-glass structure located on South Winton Road in Rochester, has become a symbol of support, comfort, and life enhancement for hundreds of Rochester families, who know that when they and their loved ones need care in their later years, a real home will be waiting for them. Situated on more than 20 grassy acres of land, the Home now provides comfort, care, extensive programming, and companionship

The present Jewish Home of Rochester, located at 2021 Winton Road South (1985).

for 362 residents, many of whom could not survive without its supportive environment. People are drawn to the Home by its communal spirit, state-of-the-art resources, and the quality of life it provides.

Originally established exclusively for members of the Jewish community, a number of the residents today are non-Jewish. About 80 percent of all residents suffer from debilitating ailments, such as strokes and Alzheimer's disease, and need round-the-clock nursing care. The others are relatively self-sufficient and suffer from more minor ailments usually associated with the aging process.

The Jewish Home grew directly out of the Jewish community of Rochester, which began in the early 1800s when a few enterprising individuals, most of them immigrants from Central Europe, ventured here to make new lives for themselves. At the time, Rochester was a vital mill and trading town in upstate New York fed by the waters of the Genesee River. Immigrants would hear about it on board ship or as soon as they arrived in New York City.

Meyer Greentree, an immigrant from Germany, was one of the first Jews to arrive in Rochester. Starting his journey in New England, he followed the westward migration of many others and, in 1843, settled in Rochester and got a job in the dry goods store of Sigmund Rosenberg, another early Jewish settler. After marrying, Greentree joined his new bride as the proprietors of a shop for manufacturing children's clothing on Front Street. In 1848, Joseph and Gabriel Wile joined the shop and formed Greentree and Wile, laying the foundation for the ready-made garment trade in Rochester, an industry that would be run almost exclusively by German-Jewish immigrants, who would dominate the local economy to the end of the century.

By the mid-1860s, twelve of the thirteen leading clothing firms in Rochester were owned partly or completely by German Jews. By 1880, the industry employed a greater number of workers than any other enterprise in town and included some leading factories such as Michaels Stern and Company, L. Adler Brothers and Company, Hays and Brothers, Schwarz Brothers, Stein-Block and Company, Levy-Adler, H.C. Cohn and Company, and Hickey-Freeman, to name a few.

In 1875, there were 3,000 Jews in Rochester, and almost all were German born. Originally they settled in the Joseph Avenue area, bounded by Central, Clifford, Clinton and Hudson avenues, a two- to three-square-mile corner of the oldest section of the city bordering the towering escarpment that is the east bank of the Genesee River. As the Jews

Country Store at the Counter, *below, is a watercolor painting by* *Barbara Moore* *on display* *at the Jewish* *Home.*

became more successful, they moved from this neighborhood to more elegant homes in the southern and eastern reaches of the city near Park Avenue, and Oxford, Barrington and Alexander streets.

In the mid-1800s, they established a house of worship, Temple Berith Kodesh (changed to B'rith Kodesh around 1905), on Gibbs Street. By the end of the century, this was one of the leading Reform temples in America. Influenced by the German Jews who were leaders in the Reform movement then sweeping America, these forward-looking settlers introduced many reforms into the religious service, including conducting services in German and later in English rather than Hebrew, playing organ music, praying without a head covering and seating men and women together in the sanctuary.

As they cast off many of the more restrictive conventions of Orthodoxy, these German Jews also maintained a lively social life, which was as integrated with the Christian community as the prevailing anti-Semitic attitudes would allow. Many became prominent civic leaders, entering politics and the professions, and sent their children to universities.

The Community Grows

This tightly knit community, however, was soon dwarfed by the wave of Eastern European Jews who began emigrating to America between 1881 and 1924. During this period, nearly 2.4 million Jews left Eastern Europe. About 12,000 found their way to Rochester, many drawn by accounts of the thriving garment industry and opportunities for employment in the Flour City. By 1890, the influx of Russian and Polish-born Jews increased the total Jewish population in

P o p u l a t i o n C o m p a r i s o n			
Date	**City of Rochester**	**Monroe County**	**Jewish**
1880	89,000	144,903	3,000
1890	125,000	189,586	5,000
1910	218,149	283,212	11,000
1920	295,750	352,084	15,000
1924	313,578		16,000
1930	328,132	423,881	17,000
1940	324,975	438,230	18,000
1960	318,611	587,387	21,000 [1]
1980	241,741	702,238	22,500 [2]
1990	231,636	713,968	22,500 [3]
1996	231,170 [4]	721,997 [4]	25,000 [4]

[1] In 1960, 37 percent of Rochester's Jews lived in the suburbs.
[2] In 1980, 76 percent of Rochester's Jews lived in the suburbs.
[3] In 1990, 85 percent of Rochester's Jews lived in the suburbs.
[4] These are population estimates.
Information for this chart was compiled by the principal author.

Rochester to about 5,000. By 1911, there were over 11,000 Jews in the city, only 2,000 of whom were German-born. By 1920, the Jewish population increased to 15,000—still a result of the flight of Jews from Eastern Europe—and stabilized at around 16,000 in 1924, when new immigration laws established strict quotas. The Jewish community in Rochester has grown slowly since that time, reaching approximately 21,000 in 1950 and 25,000 in 1995.

The new immigrants from Eastern Europe repeated the cycle of the German Jews, settling in the Joseph Avenue area of Rochester. These new settlers worked as tailors, cutters or pressers in large factories, living and working in an area dominated by breweries, gas works, warehouses and the cascading falls of the Genesee River. For the most part, these new settlers were young, single, unskilled and poorly educated, but boundlessly optimistic. Some had come to America seeking their fortune in the *goldene medina* (the "golden country"). Others were fleeing

the cruel pogroms and oppressive policies of czarist Russia, Lithuania, Poland and Galicia. Some had grown up in *shtetlach* (villages), while others had grown up in large cities.

Religious Ties

These differences created a smorgasbord of dialects, customs and habits as well as a proliferation of synagogues, each created to sustain the rituals and styles of the different *minhagim* (religious customs). By 1900, there were six Orthodox congregations in Rochester; by 1925, there were eleven more, creating a total of 17 different Orthodox synagogues in the small city. These synagogues included Beth Israel Congregation (the Leopold Street Shul), Anshe Poland, Ahavas Achim, Beth Hamedresh Hagadol, Anshe Kipel Volin, Etz Chaim and Ein Jacob. Some were short lived; others, like the Beth Joseph Center, founded a bit later adjacent to the original Jewish Home site, have a long history.

Ellis Island, *an oil on canvas painting by Helen Smagorinski. From the Jewish Home art collection.*

4

Despite these differences, all shared the simple Orthodoxy and traditions of *Yiddishkeyt* (Jewishness), as well as a history of deprivation and suffering. They all knew what it meant to be a Jew. Their *shules* were not simply composed of like-minded believers joined together for public worship; they were gathering places where recent immigrants could fashion a fellowship-community. As a *kehillah* (community), they extended care and a helping hand to their members, offering them visits during sickness, proper Jewish burials and assistance during hard times. They provided members with a sense of security and status, a safe harbor to which they could return for prayer and sociability after navigating the often stormy waters of everyday economic life. In so doing, these synagogues became havens, promulgating the ethic and commitment that would eventually motivate Jews to found a home that would take care of the elderly.

Getting an Education

This was truly a remarkable generation. These new immigrants plunged into creating conditions that would allow them to survive as Jews and as fledgling Americans with a passion, a sense of urgency and a sense of humor that would sustain them, the institutions they founded, and future generations. Those who wanted an education sought out night schools run by the Rochester Board of Education. So strong was the demand that five evening schools were set up primarily for new immigrants. By 1922, 50 percent of the adult students in School No. 9 were Eastern European Jews and 25 percent of the students in School No. 18 were as well. The Baden Street Settlement offered an even wider range of courses and

services in a more *heimishe* (homelike) atmosphere. In their eagerness to learn, these immigrants formed a remarkable group—curious and ambitious, if somewhat naive. Their energy found expression in a myriad of political and cultural organizations as well as the burgeoning trade unions they formed and joined. Yiddish was the language of discourse in all of them.

Theirs was also a passionate society, a world reinventing itself—without much support from the German-Jewish community, which had a different language, culture, religious orientation, class and ethos. Instead of receiving help from these earlier Jewish settlers, the newly arrived immigrants depended on neighbors, friends, *landslayt* (countrymen), and the deeply imbued traditions of self-help and mutual responsibility to get them through the tough times like the dreaded slow seasons of the garment industry.

Their pleasures took place within their world. Yiddish theater was brought to local theaters by Max Fogel, the father of Harriet Lewis, a dedicated volunteer activist and president of the Jewish Home's Ladies Auxiliary (1981-83). Fogel laughed and wallowed with his fellow Jews in nostalgia. As there seemed to be a *shul* or *landsmanshaft* group for every town in Eastern Europe, these institutions became substitute families where members could hear the accents of home, share memories and help out in times of need. As a generation, they were intensely social and enjoyed themselves at card parties, lectures, or a meal at Cohen's delicatessen, where they perfected the healing power of talk and a *gloz té* (a glass of tea).

Throughout these years, the Jewish community was marked by a sense of involvement, a constant ferment of causes,

convictions and caring, where Socialists, Bundists, Zionists, anti-Zionists and Yiddishists engaged in constant intellectual debate.

Joseph Avenue

Joseph Avenue was Rochester's version of New York City's Delancey Street or Chicago's Maxwell Street. It started at Central Avenue, the edge of the downtown area, and dipped under the bridge carrying the New York Central railroad tracks. Community life tended to revolve around the ten-block ribbon of little stores and businesses in this area, which were mostly owned by Jews, where the food was kosher and where there was a meat market on every corner. The stores provided all services and goods. Nusbaum's Department Store sold a bit of everything; Levy's and Cook's repaired worn shoes; Gissin Electric sold bulbs, fixtures and electrical supplies; Orgel's and Tillim's sold religious articles and dry goods; Kolko's tailor shop sold threads and cloth; Carl Lawrence provided herring; Amdursky's, Applebaum's, Goldman's and Cohen's sold kosher meats and chicken; Naditz's bakery specialized in freshly baked pumpernickel breads; Quality Bakery, New York Bakery, Sands', Bodner's and Gottfried's produced baked goods with a European *tam* (flavor); and Simon's Creamery and Danishefsky's Dairy were replete with fresh butter, farmer cheese, lox and other delicacies.

During the next twenty-five years, this situation changed as many of these Eastern European Jews repeated the path of their predecessors. As they became more acclimated to American life, often discarding their peddler's pack and working in factories as skilled needle-trade workers, they learned new skills and trades.

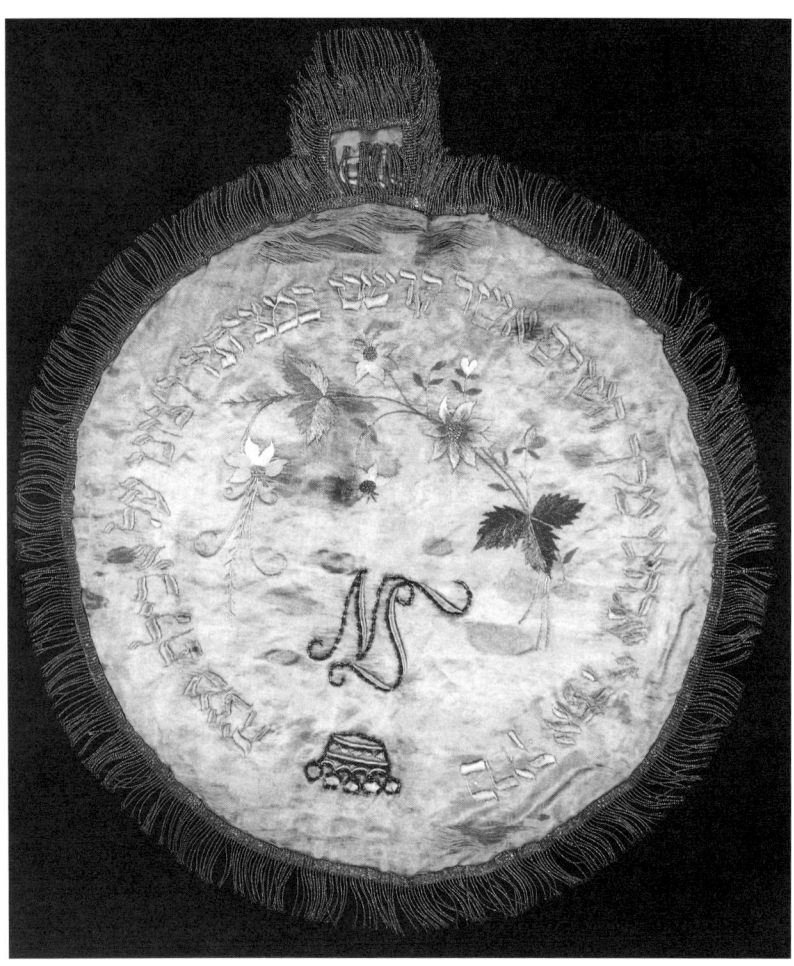

Antique Matzo Cover *from the Jewish Home of Rochester art collection.*

Many could save enough money to start businesses and become proprietors of small stores, or to be wholesalers or managers. Many sent their children to East High School, and some of these graduates went on to university study.

Community and *Tzedakah*

People belonged to charitable organizations; women were prominent in this work. Fund-raising was ongoing; there was always a raffle or fund-raising event supporting a cause, as well as the omnipresent *pushke* (charity box).

As *Yiddishkeyt* in America became less tragic and less a sorrowful remembrance, it became more characterized by affirmation. It did not matter to these new Jewish settlers that they were drifting slowly from the beliefs and practices they had brought from their homelands and that new rituals were gradually remaking their holidays and traditions. What counted was their irreducible sense of community, the expressiveness of their own language, the sights and smells of their neighborhood and the sense of responsibility they felt for their own.

A *yid*, they said, *blaybt a yid*. A Jew remains a Jew. Be they orphaned, impoverished, sick or elderly, they must be taken care of with dignity and in the proper Jewish spirit. That is the ethos, the obligation of *tzedakah*—righteousness and charity—which was

to inspire those who founded the Jewish Home of Rochester. For many of these Jews, charity was and still is the very heart of Judaism. The rituals of religion could be diverse and even divisive, split among Orthodox, Conservative and Reform Jews, and the communities of German and Eastern European Jews were often at odds. Despite these differences, the spirit of *tzedakah* united everyone, because accomplishing good works was an incontestable goal. *Tzedakah*, after all, means more than passive charity. It involves actively caring, doing what you can for others, doing even more than you think you can. It was this shared sense of *tzedakah*—taking care of your own—that inspired the original founders of the Jewish Home as well as those who have worked over the many decades to make it the impressive community resource it has become.

As early as 1882, for example, the German Jews in Rochester founded the United Jewish Charities to help the needy in their neighborhoods. Thirty years later, the Eastern European Jews decided to establish their own philanthropy, the Associated Hebrew Charities, to aid their own people. Under the leadership of men like Lester Nusbaum, the first president of the Home, the Associated made such progress that in the summer of 1913, it was able to complete the construction of its own building at 144 Baden Street. It was also in this period that thought for the welfare of the aged and infirm began in earnest. In 1910, all the groups affiliated with the Associated were involved. There were plans to build a home at the intersection of Nassau and Joiner streets, in the heart of the Jewish neighborhood. Initially little came of this plan. A small group of women organized themselves as the Bikur Cholim Society, which provided nursing care for the sick. The women diligently began to set aside funds over the next eight years. When they had amassed several thousand dollars, they began systematically to pressure a number of the leaders of the community to join them in this project. In 1918, the Jewish Home for the Aged came into being and was incorporated on March 20, 1920.

The Jewish Home stands out as an exception to the patterns previously noted in the Rochester Jewish community. Because the problem of poverty among the aged was not nearly as serious among the earlier German settlers, they did not evidence an interest in setting up such an institution. Since the Reform group was not particularly interested in keeping kosher laws, that would not have been one of their priorities. In the field of social responsibility, however, no active antagonism existed between the

two communities. At first the German Jewish community was not involved in a major way, but after several decades this tentative support was transformed into major commitment. The Home gradually became a community resource that belonged to everyone. It was built in Jewish neighborhoods, first on St. Paul Street and later in Brighton, to serve Jewish requirements in fulfillment of their long-standing obligation to care for the elderly and those in need.

Substantial as it now seems, the institution that began modestly at 1162 St. Paul Street in the immigrant section was established with hardly a glance at the impression it would make in the general community. Like the *mitzvah* of charity itself that is to be given anonymously, without fanfare, and always with the benefit of the recipient in mind, the Jewish Home has achieved its reputation quietly

and with dignity. As Will Greenberg, the director of the Home from 1957 to 1984, recalled: "The mission of providing for our elderly in a proper Jewish setting has never changed. The Jewish Home was a community place from day one. The family is the center. The Home is the extension of the Jewish family." There hardly is a Jewish family in Rochester that has not been touched by it.

In the following pages we will tell its story, the remarkable story of its dedicated cadre of lay supporters and professionals, men and women of vision, courage and caring, who have made the Home one of Rochester's most cherished resources.

Schoen Alley,
a painting by
Thomas Miller.
From the Jewish
Home of Rochester
art collection.

"The mission of providing for our elderly in a proper Jewish setting has never changed. The Jewish Home was a community place from day one. The family is the center. The Home is the extension of the Jewish family."

Sabbath, *a serigraph by Pinchas Shaar, is on display at the Jewish Home of Rochester. It is a gift from family in memory of Bernie Shapiro.*

Will Greenberg

chapter one

Making a Home

"Cast me not off
in time of old age
when my strength faileth."

P s a l m s

1920 - 1934

Residents light a menorah in the Jewish Home synagogue during the 1920s (at right).

The sign below, in English and Hebrew, is from first site of the Jewish Home at 1162 St. Paul Street.

"Ladies, I have something to ask you. Every city has a Jewish home except Rochester. How come?"

Gitel Cohen, about 1918, quoted by daughter Reva Rock

Humble Beginnings

Prior to 1920, many elderly people in Rochester—Jews and non-Jews alike—led a perilous and fragile existence, dependent upon the goodwill of relatives and neighbors to help them perform the most minimal daily chores. The more fortunate remained self-sufficient until their final days. Others suffered from dementia or other crippling diseases and had no family able to care for them or money to hire help. Their only alternative was the County Hospital, an anonymous and understaffed public institution that had no provisions for religious rituals and little sense of community or warmth. Within its stony walls, it was impossible for Jewish residents even to light a Sabbath candle. Early records document cases of Orthodox residents who were so unhappy there that they starved themselves by refusing to eat non-kosher food.

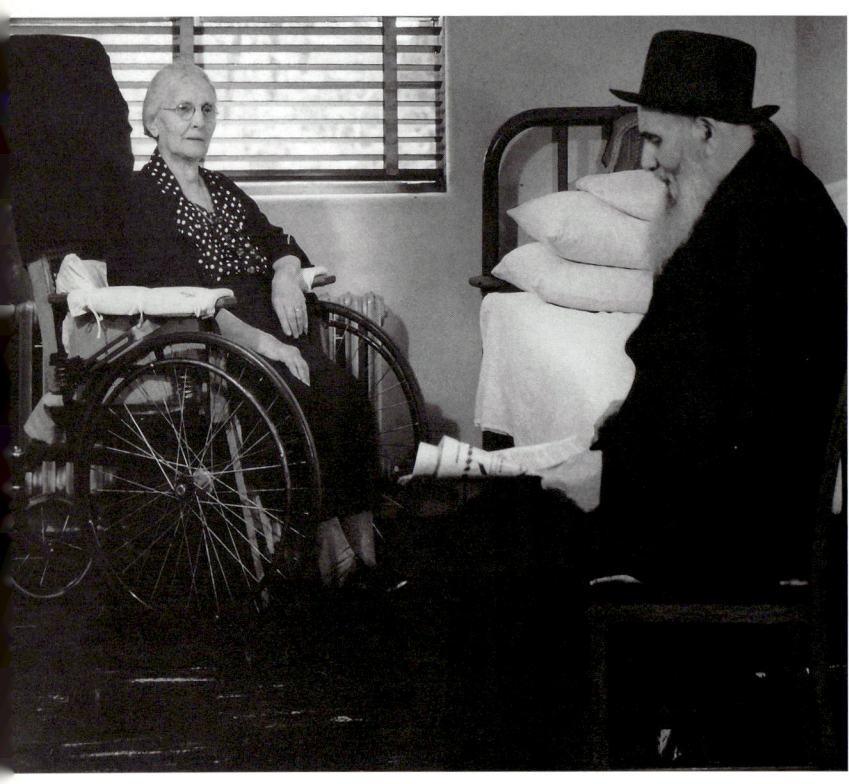

Elderly couples could stay together during the time they needed each other the most. Family centered from its beginning, the Jewish Home distinguished itself in the 1920s as one of few homes for the aged that allowed married people.

selected the site
for the Home
on 1162 St.
Paul Street, a
$15,000 house
on a good-size

Jewish neighbor-
hood. The Board
closed the deal
on September 1,
1920.

The Board of Charities grants a charter to Rochester's Jewish Home for the Aged on February 10.

Rochester's Jewish Home for the Aged incorporates on March 20.

A meeting of Rochester's Jews is held in the Associated Hebrew Charities Building on Baden Street, attracting 300 people who donate $832.

Representatives of the ten Rochester *shuls* arrange fund-raising campaign for the Jewish Home on Yom Kippur, which yields $22,850 in donations.

Daughters of the Jewish Home for the Aged forms.

The Board decides to admit only people over 60.

Monroe County has 352,034 residents.

America experiences almost a decade of unbridled economic expansion and speculation.

Making a Home

Founding Mothers

Mrs. Gitel Cohen, a short, dark-haired woman born in Eastern Europe, was acutely aware of the dire fate awaiting many of these elderly Jews, since she and other women in the Jewish community, who had organized the Bikur Cholim Society, would visit those who didn't have nearby family on Fridays and help them prepare for the Sabbath. Fearing that these elderly shut-ins, and even members of her

Brina Appelbaum (left)

own family, might be forced to travel this terrifying route at a time in life when they would be the most vulnerable, she called four friends— Mrs. Cohen, Mrs. Meyer Amdursky, Mrs. Brina Appel-baum (the grandmother of Jean Natapow), and Mrs. Sarah Meyer—to a meeting at her home in 1918. As her daughter Reva Rock later

On February 1, 1921, say the Board minutes, "Doors opened and the first seven residents were admitted— two men and five women." By 1924, the Home would become a jewel in Rochester's Jewish community, with more than 30 residents and hundreds of supporters.

The JEWISH LEDGER

Published Weekly in the Interest of Roches

RELIGION

Dinner to Mark Formal Opening of New Home

recalled, Gitel Cohen began with a direct question: "Ladies," she said, "I have something to ask you. Every city has a Jewish home except Rochester. How come?"

Jewish homes for the aged in America began to be established in the late 1850s. They evolved when it became apparent that the needs of many frail elderly could not be adequately met through existing family arrangements, given the precarious economic

position that many of these recent immigrants experienced. Institutional care for the Jewish aged in America began in 1855 in St. Louis, and took the form of large boarding homes in which elderly Jews could retire in a relatively safe environment. Few, if any, medical or social services were provided. Operating expenses were derived from fees paid by residents

and the charity dollars collected from the community. This is the model that Gitel Cohen probably had in mind when she implored her friends for assistance. This remarkable group of founders, however, would soon display the vision and commitment that has characterized the leadership of the Home ever

The Jewish Ledger

December 12, 192_

Page Two

Where Happiness Rules the Twilight of Life

HOW BUILDINGS AND GROUNDS OF THE JEWISH HOME FOR THE AGED APPEAR TODAY

Rochester's Aged Jewry "Have Not Been Forsaken;" Institution Here Boasts Facilities Comparable with Best in the United States; Will Dedicate New Modern Addition Sunday

SUNDAY will be a red letter day in the history of the Jewish Home for the Aged, No. 1162 St. Paul Street, for on that day will be marked the completion of the new addition and the renovation of the entire property, at a cost of $50,000. Open house will be observed in the afternoon, and in the evening at 6.30 o'clock a dinner will be given for 300 guests, at which _ _ _ _ Toronto, a

might endanger such a happy condition.

Had Spiritual Foundation

Jewish Home for the Ag_ _

brated by a banquet at whi
prominent Jews were present
Soon after it was reporte
Board that the adjoining Fee
was to be sold and in order
the future expansion of the
resolution was adopted autho
officers to purchase the pr
$22,500. This property has
of 220 feet and a depth o
Only as mall balance was i
ury at the time, and Solo_
a member of the Board
$1,000 to make the initial
the property which was p

since. They moved rapidly during several decades, from the modest objective of care-taking to an institution that offered better care for the dependent elderly than could be found elsewhere in the public or private domain. The Home was to be characterized by the highest standards of medical attention and social and recreational program-ming, and was always infused with a *Yiddishe tam* (Yiddish feeling).

The women proceeded to look into possibilities of setting up a home for the aged in Rochester. They soon located a large frame house at 1162 St. Paul Street with enough bedrooms for seven full-time residents and several support personnel. The house was within easy walking distance of the nearby Orthodox community, where most Jews still lived. But it cost $15,000, at that time a large sum of money. Since women in those days could not arrange financing on their own, they went to Lester Nusbaum, a successful furrier and devout Jew, and asked him to help them. Nusbaum, a skilled businessman with a strong loyalty to the Jewish community, became involved immediately. After obtaining a bank mortgage to underwrite the cost of buying the home, he organized a group of 35 men and women to serve on

the Board of Directors. The Bikur Cholim Society donated $4,000 from its treasury to the Home.

When the Board met for the first time, on August 17, 1920, Nusbaum was elected president, a role he would carry out with passion, energy and intelligence for the next 22 years. The Board empow-ered him to purchase the prop-erty at 1162 St. Paul Street. Other original officers included William Brown, Mrs. T. Goldman, Mrs. R. Gold-stein, Frank Sherman, Joseph E. Silverstein, Anna Wolfe, and M. M. Gallant. Dr. Jacob S. Kominz, a Rochester physi-cian, was elected house physi-cian, and Maurice G. Ellenbogen was asked to provide legal services. A women's auxiliary group, The Daughters of the Jewish Home (also known as The Daughters Club), was set up to provide volunteer services.

The first board began to draw up bylaws and plans for the comfort of its residents, making city residency, suffi-cient age (60 or older), and urgent need primary require-ments. They would guide all their actions, Lester Nusbaum and the Board members pledged, by the vision of the Home's founders "that it should be a real Home in every way, and that our atti-tude toward the aged should be one of sympathy."

Word about the new Home went out initially at a meeting held on September 5, 1920, in the Associated Hebrew Chari-ties Building on Baden Street. About 300 people attended, and addresses of support were made by Rabbis J. S. Minkin, Horace J. Wolf and Solomon Levin. The community showed support in the form of every kind of donation—from clothing to food to furniture. People gave money and offered to help with recreation and religious activities. A *siyum hatorah* (completion of the Torah) would bring in $196. Seven Rochester syna-gogues had appeals on Yom Kippur to support the Home, a practice that continued for a number of years. They also helped the Home form a *minyan* (prayer quorum), so it could have its own synagogue. By the end of the year, almost $25,000 was raised and the mortgage on 1162 St. Paul Street was completely paid off.

First Residents

By January 23, 1921, the Home was ready for a triumphant dedication. Frank Sherman, the Home's first treasurer, hired two cars to "bring the old folks to the Home"—two men and five women, immigrants from Eastern Europe and Germany who spoke little English and had no immediate family members who could take care

The Jewish Home's First Board of Directors

*The Board held its
first meeting, with
21 members present.
President Lester Nusbaum
outlined their duties
and responsibilities to
create "the ideal Home
of the City of Rochester."
These names are given as
they appear in the Board
Minutes of 1921.*

Lester Nusbaum
President

William Brown *1st Vice President*	Joseph E. Silverstein *Recording Secretary*
Mrs. T. Goldman *2nd Vice President*	Anna Wolfe *Financial Secretary*
Mrs. R. Goldstein *3rd Vice President*	William Brown *Chairman of House Committee*
Frank Sherman *Treasurer*	M. M. Gallant *Chairman of Applications*

Board of Directors:

Louis Shulman	Israel Schoenberg	J. Z. Braveman
Abraham Davidson	Mrs. J. S. Minkin	M. M. Gallant
Mrs. M. Amdursky	Mrs. L. A. Olsan	Haskell H. Marks
Mrs. M. Appelbaum	Chas. Messinger	A. Alderman
Lester Goldstein	David Harrison	K. Pliskin
Louis Simon	Nathan Kaplan	Sol Levin
Abraham Goldman	Lester Paley	Abe Barnett
Dr. J. S. Kominz	Hyman Goldman	M. Fauman
	Max Cohen	Mrs. J. Gordon

1921 continued

The Board pays off an $8,000 balance and burns the mortgage.

The Home purchases property located at 1180 St. Paul Street from Mrs. John C. Fee for $22,500; contribution of $1,000 given by Sol Levin.

Superintendent Matilda Roseman reports that the "spirit of the House was very good, and the health of the people was good." She suggests that a committee for recreation and amusement be appointed.

The Board sends a letter to the Community Chest requesting funds.

The cost per resident is $13.65 a week.

1922

The Board appoints Dr. Jacob S. Kominz chairman of the medical staff. Five other physicians volunteer to assist him.

Prohibition takes effect. Rochester's city court convicts the first local speakeasy proprietor.

of them. On February 1, 1921, they were driven up to the front door and welcomed by a buoyant group of board members, volunteers and reporters. For many, it was their first ride in an automobile. Donations from the Jewish community continued to come in, ranging from soda water and dry cleaning services to fresh fruit and vegetables and medicine.

Dr. Kominz, the uncle of future Jewish Home board member and leader Bob Weinberg, although busy with a practice of his own, organized a team of volunteer medical doctors and aides. At the same time, The Daughters Club expanded rapidly, gathering hundreds of volunteers who gave linens, dishes and clothing to the Home and made weekly visits to residents.

The men soon settled into a comfortable routine, reading Yiddish newspapers like the *Forvorts* (Forward) or *Der Tog* (The Day), and studying the Talmud. The women would sew, knit, gossip heatedly and listen to records. In the evenings, they all ate kosher meals together and played gin rummy. On Friday night and Saturday mornings,

they attended religious services in a synagogue created in the basement of the Home. "Inmates enjoy a cozy and congenial life in an atmosphere and surroundings different from those of ordinary institutions," reported an article in the *Rochester Democrat & Chronicle*, titled "Where Life's Twilight Is Made Happy."

As the Home became a coveted refuge in the community, many local charities, ranging from the Aleph Eien Club for young men to the Junior Jewish Council, volunteered help and support, often visiting residents and entertaining them with musical programs and readings. Fundraising became a main activity of the Board. Donors who supported the Home with annual gifts of $6.00 were designated "members." Donors pledging more were designated "sponsors."

Just seven months after the first residents moved in, the Home purchased the house next door, at 1180 St. Paul Street. Interest in the Home was growing. The men lived in the new house; the women and dining facilities stayed in the old. But the arrangement proved difficult for the men, some of whom had trouble crossing the yard to get their meals in nasty winter weather. More money was needed to expand. In September 1923,

Solomon Snider and Irving Bieber supervised a major capital campaign, raising an impressive $40,000 at a gala dinner held at the Seneca Hotel. In December 1924, an addition was opened that provided not only shelter from one end of the residence to the other, but space for more beds, bringing the count eventually to 65.

A Home Away from Home

As the Home grew in size and reputation, more and more programs were added to provide residents with a sense of community and Jewish tradition. The National Council of Jewish Women held a Sunday School there, and a committee was formed to supervise and facilitate closer family relationships. In January 1923, the Home bought its first piano, the result of a major gift from a local card-playing group.

"The Jewish Home for the Aged, I am convinced, is already a notable achievement and it has given opportunity to many dear souls to spend their remaining days in blessedness and contentment," wrote Nellie Kahn, when she donated $500 in memory of her husband. Other major donors of the time included Mr. and Mrs. Frank Sherman, who endowed the main hall for $1,000. Their grandchildren are presently very

A resident blows the shofar before the open ark in the Jewish Home's synagogue. Members of the Jewish community used the synagogue and Home for important events, such as weddings and bar mitzvahs.

involved in the Home, demonstrating links of continuity between generations.

Open Doors for the Infirm

By 1925, there were 30 residents in the Home and a growing list of applicants, along with hundreds of supporters. Bylaws were amended in January 1926, empowering the Board "to make arrangements for the care of the aged infirm Jews." This was a major change of policy, a responsibility many other homes for the aged did not accept. As this population of infirm and partly disabled began to come to the Home, Dr. Jacob S. Kominz realized the need to formalize the organization of the volunteer medical staff. He worked with respected Jewish physicians in general practice, including Drs. Nathan W. Soble, Sol J. Appelbaum, J. Berkman and Isadore Hurwitz, and ophthalmologists like Dr. Macy Lerner, who generously took time from their own busy practices to provide services gratis and to set standards for medical care at the Home. They adopted bylaws that required doctors to visit at least once each week and "as often as necessary to properly

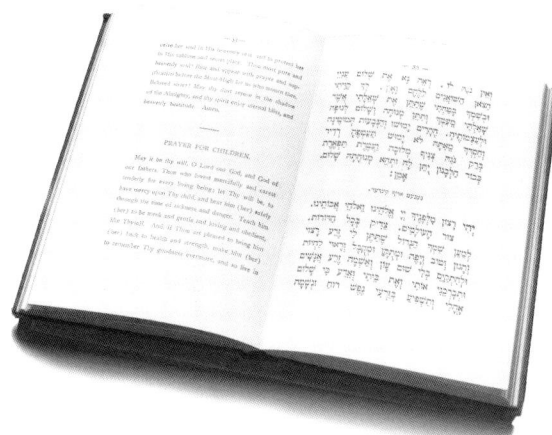

Families donated many objects to the synagogue; items from Torah covers to prayer books are inscribed in their memory.

Joseph E. Silverstein, an insurance salesman, volunteered in the early 1920s to lead religious services. He prayed and read with residents every Saturday and holidays until the 1980s.

Mr. Silverstein benefited spiritually from his service at the Home and in other ways, says daughter Bea Silverstein Frank; he met and married the Home's first superintendent, Margaret Goldberg. The man standing is Samuel Krawetz, superintendent of the Home from 1932 to 1946.

*Ritual obser-
vances at the
Home were an
important part
of the activities
of the residents.*

23

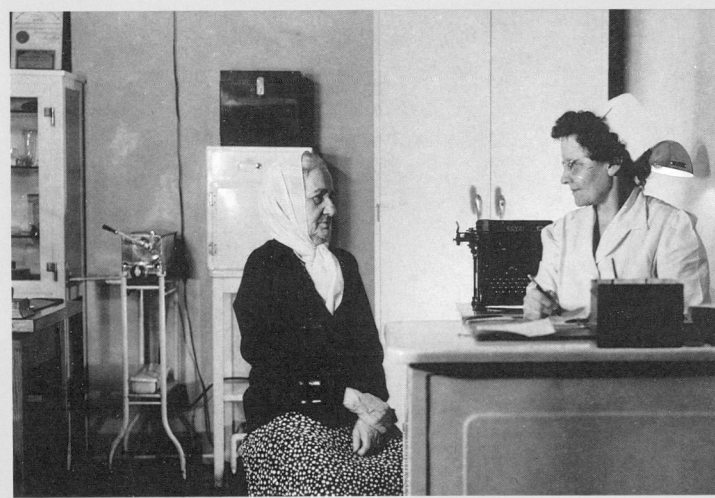

The Home depended on a volunteer medical staff throughout the 1920s, and residents enjoyed the best care available.

Medical staff minutes describe doctors' use of the latest medical developments on patients.

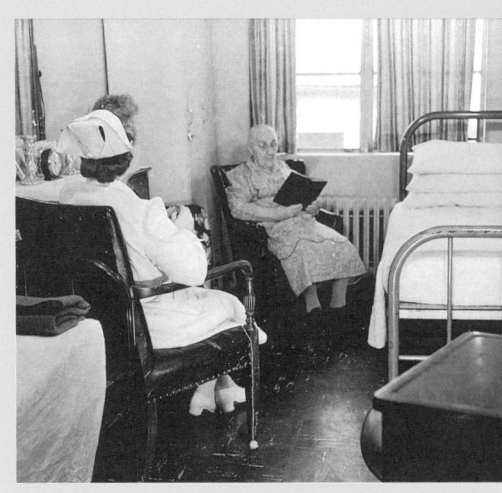

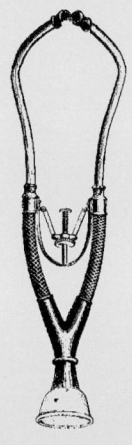

"Members of the Staff shall give their services gratis to all inmates of the Home, at any time." Minutes of the Medical Staff, February 14, 1929.

care for patients," and to "visit cases demanding urgent treatment as soon as possible after receiving notice." To reflect these changes, the Board changed the name from The Jewish Home for the Aged to The Jewish Home for the Aged and the Infirm Aged. The Home was also among the first in the nation to accept married couples.

Tradition

While many in the community worked to make the Home a meaningful experience, several individuals made contributions that are still talked about today. Joseph Silverstein, a young insurance salesman and Orthodox Jew, lived nearby on Avenue B. He was deeply committed to assuring that the Home would provide for the religious needs of the residents. For more than 60 years, he walked to the Home every Friday night and twice on Saturday, and on all the holidays, to conduct services for the residents with his wonderful voice.

Silverstein, who eventually became vice mayor and comptroller of the City of Rochester, also sat on the original board that hired Margaret Goldberg, from Tennessee, as chief nurse. Margaret turned out to be so effective that she was soon promoted to superintendent. But residents were not the only ones charmed by her

skills and generous spirit; Joe himself was smitten. "Legend has it that he questioned whether a woman could do the job of superintendent," recalled his daughter, Bea Silverstein Frank, a professor of law at New York University, at the dedication of the Joseph E. Silverstein Memorial Court on September 15, 1991. "But he soon learned that she could do the job better than anyone had done it before and he then offered her another position—spouse."

Joe and Margaret were married on August 15, 1926, in the Home. (Years later, Bea Silverstein married her husband, Lloyd Frank, in the very same synagogue, and her brother David, a physician, had his bar mitzvah there.) "My father would visit residents after morning prayers," she recalled fondly. "With some he discussed the news of the day, with others he recited prayers. He brought the outside world and the comforts of religion to those who were unable to leave their rooms. In his understanding of the needs of the residents—an understanding shared by and perhaps learned from my mother—he was ahead of his time. He knew instinctively what social workers and other human services professionals go to school to learn."

By 1927, there were 49 residents in the Home (25 women and 24 men),

including two married couples, four totally disabled residents and nine residents who were partially disabled. Two-thirds of the group received financial subsidies of some kind. While the Board made efforts to take care of people with manageable ailments, it also set up arrangements with nearby hospitals to transfer patients who became critically ill. Residents, however, were not always ready to accept these transfers. When one elderly woman fell and was sent to Strong Memorial Hospital for treatment, she was so unhappy that she refused to eat the hospital food and insisted on returning to the Home.

For most residents, the Home was not an impersonal institution, but a family where they lived, learned and prayed together. They enjoyed frequent Purim parties, Hanukkah celebrations, Passover seders and Sabbath services, along with piano recitals and birthday celebrations. As cars became more available, volunteers took residents on frequent outings. Corbett's Glen in Brighton and Summerville by Lake Ontario were favorites.

In 1928, Rabbi and Mrs. Morris Goldman became the new superintendent and matron of the Home. Soon after, plans were developed to start an infirmary that would provide specialized care for

1922 continued
"Learn English" classes in Rochester attract 2,183 new immigrants.

The Home is admitted to the Community Chest.

Rochester's first commercial radio station WHQ (later WHEC) gets 26th broadcasting license issued in United States (623 licensed stations in 1938).

Brina [Mrs. A.] Appelbaum reports that new dresses were being made for the women for the holidays and all other necessary clothing was being bought.

The National Council of Jewish Women begin holding Sunday School at the Home.

Mrs. Horowitz and Rabbi Minkin recommend that a permanent committee "known as the Arbitration or Rehabilitation committee be

appointed to bring a closer relationship between husband and wife and parents and children."

1923
The Home rents the garage at 1180 St. Paul to be used as Hebrew school and *shul*.

The Bridgette Club presents a check for $117 to the Home, the net receipts of a card party. The money is used to help pay for a piano that costs $275.

The B'nai B'rith Hillel Foundation is established at the University of Illinois at Urbana.

the disabled elderly—a facility that would eventually make the Home distinctive as most other homes for the aged did not provide advanced medical care for people with serious conditions.

Hard Times

But these and other plans came to a halt when the stock market crashed in 1929. The Home was not spared the financial pain that struck all other institutions. The Depression hit the Jewish community in Rochester quite hard. It threatened the viability of the vast network of social welfare, cultural and religious institutions Jews had created to serve their needs. Maintaining voluntary organizations in an economic crisis is low in priority for a family that needs food, rent or mortgage payments. The Community Chest, now known as United Way, cut its allocations to the Home three years in a row. As donations from community members dwindled and the deficit rose, the Board had to cut back needed services and institute various precautions. The superintendent had to cut already modest wages.

Desperate people who came asking for food would still be fed, but because the night guard had been laid off, they would be served outside. The medical staff had to scavenge for medication, putting insulin and heart medicine on the top of the list and foregoing other, less critical, ones they could no longer afford.

The Board, composed of dedicated and courageous individuals like Morris Rosenbloom, Samuel Ball, and Allen Eber, made repeated pleas for a new addition to the Home to relieve overcrowding and to provide refuge for the elderly suffering at the County Hospital or in stressed family situations. They were advised by Dr. Kominz and other medical experts that as more bedridden and sick individuals were seeking the Home's care, an infirmary to accommodate this growing population was needed. "If we went back to the limited task of just taking care of the well aged we would not be doing a good job," he said. An architect would plan, set a budget and then face the disappointment that funds were not available. Still, the energetic Lester Nusbaum refused to give up

plans for expansion when he was told by a local charity to save money by refusing "infirm cases." That was not the Jewish way.

Recovery

In 1936, when the economy slowly began to come back, aided by massive federal programs like Social Security, the Home's fortunes began to rise again. A new fund-raising drive chaired by Benjamin Forman, founder of B. Forman Co., and Hattie Neisner, wife of the founder of Neisner Brothers, produced $45,000—enough to complete the infirmary. A glowing article in *The Democrat & Chronicle* on August 10, 1936, noted that "the Jewish Home is among the first old age organizations in the country to accept chronically ill as well as healthy old people." It had been doing so since 1925. "The new one-story brick structure is fire-proof and will have a completely outfitted medical room, examining room, solarium with x-ray and sun lamps, and special conveniences for the blind and crippled patients." This 27-bed facility was dedicated on January 3, 1937.

The cost per resident is $15 a week. Rochester's coal supply is cut 40 percent because of shortage. The Home and many others burn coke.

The capital surplus budget is $2,250.92. Rabbi Minkin informs the Jewish community of the Home's need for money to enlarge the Home and accommodate waiting applicants. Building campaign drive begins.

Temple B'rith Kodesh has 75th anniversary.

The Home mourns the death of President Warren Harding and holds special services in his memory. Lester Nusbaum and A. B. Goldman become Rochester's representatives to the American

Jewish Congress, and the Rochester branch elects Mr. Nusbaum as president.

The Board calls a public meeting at Associated Hebrew Charities and begins effort to connect its two buildings.

Dr. Kominz organizes the Home's volunteer medical staff. The Board appoints a Campaign Committee to raise $45,000 for the addition. Solomon Snider and Irving Bieber are joint chairmen of the campaign. They choose as architect

Sigmund Firestone, who is known for his work on the County Hospital on South Avenue, now called the Monroe Community Hospital.

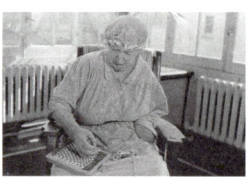

At Home

1923 continued

The Daughters Club pays for residents' dental work at Baden St. dispensary.

The Board adopts plans for 10 new rooms on the ground floor, with all modern conveniences, including a new heating system, kitchen, dining room, and sick rooms.

1924

Maurice Masor is hired to "do all services as ordered by the Superintendent and by the House Committee and Board" for $125 a month plus room and board.

The annual budget for the coming year allows for $25 in stationery, $250 for medicine, $5,600 for food, $45 for transportation, and $750 for electricity and gas.

The Sunshine Club is organized "for the purpose of entertaining the old members and in every way looking after the social welfare of the Home."

President Calvin Coolidge signs the Immigration Act of 1924, which ends the era of unrestricted immigration to the United States.

Samuel Goldwyn and Louis B. Mayer found the Metro-Goldwyn-Mayer Co.

The Community Chest reaches fund-raising goal of $2,301,068.

1925

Mr. and Mrs. Frank Sherman endow the main hall for $1,000. Mr. Nusbaum explains to the Board: "Some applicants who are poor and whose relations are poor are free. Some pay cost of board only, some pay for board plus overhead or the full cost of maintenance."

Delta Psi, a Jewish sorority at the University of Rochester, gives an informal dance to raise funds.

After discussing the "two very serious cases of Jewish women at the County Hospital," the Board resolves that officers of the Home are "empowered to made arrangements for the care of the aged infirm Jews" in that facility.

1926

Dr. Kominz moves that "the Board be empowered if no other reason intervenes to admit disabled applicants to the Jewish Home for the Aged and that physical disability other than mental or communicable diseases be no bar." Before this, patients were often sent to the County Hospital when they were seriously ill.

I Remember

Elizabeth Schwartz remembers grandmother Julia Morris, who lived at the home in 1930.

"She told us about life there—'The men opened the windows and the women closed them.' She was an active person who loved to attend services in the *shul* and to play cards and dominoes with the men. Very often, she would sit with the women, keeping busy crocheting, making doilies and placemats containing her own designs of candlesticks and menorahs. She really enjoyed the life and activities of the Home."

"We have followed along the lines laid down by the founders of this Home, that it should be a real Home in every way, and that our attitude toward the aged should be one of sympathy."

Lester Nusbaum, 9th Annual Meeting, January 19, 1926

"The Home has been successful in making the old folks happy and contented...The ideal was to establish a Home that will be a comfort...and to be conducted in the interest of the old folks only."

Lester Nusbaum, 6th Annual Meeting, January 12, 1926

1926 continued
The Home spends several months without a superintendent. A grippe epidemic takes hold in Rochester. Several residents at the Home suffer from it.

The JYMA buys new site on Andrews and North streets.

The cost per resident is $17.55 a week.

Brina Appelbaum becomes life member of the Home.

The Home changes its formal name to the Jewish Home for the Aged and Infirm Aged.

Rochester's first public showing of "talking movies" is held at the Baptist Temple.

The Home plants rose bushes and grape vines.

A Jewish Girl Scout troop entertains and serves refreshments at the Home.

Total membership of the Home is up to 1,081. Dues in May total $569.50.

The Board gives night nurse $10 raise to $65 per month.

Mr. and Mrs. Lester Nusbaum invite female residents to their summer home in Summerville in honor of their son's bar mitzvah.

The Home has 44 residents—20 women and 24 men.

Residents enjoying a favorite pastime.

The living room of the original Home on St. Paul Street.

Sun porch with desk and calendar.

The Board approves the purchase of two more fire extinguishers and a "drying machine."

Dr. Kominz begins to keep medical history sheets for all residents on their illnesses and symptoms during their stays.

The Synagogue Council of America is established.

The Jewish population of the United States is 4.1 million. The Jewish population in Rochester is 16,000.

1928
An addition connects the Home's two buildings on the second floor, providing improved quarters for the care of the chronically ill and a sun porch for residents who cannot get outside easily.

Mrs. Forman enters the Home. Her son, Benjamin, endows a room in honor of his mother for $1,000 and agrees to pay $25 per week above the actual expense of her care, plus any medical or clothing expenses.

Cases of tuberculosis occur at the Home. Carriers go to Iola Sanitarium.

The Home shows a deficit of $1,098.50.

A Mr. Levy applies to become a resident. He "wants a home among

his own people, having lived away from Jewish people for the last forty years."

The National Conference of Christians and Jews is established to combat prejudice.

When the Home needed a piano, the Ladies Auxiliary began a special fund.

Victrolas and radios also made the Home a cozier place.

Residents' social lives picked up considerably as cars became cheaper and more available during the 1920s. Minutes record two-hour rides around Rochester, with gifts of cigars for the men to puff as they saw the city as never before. The Daughters Club, who provided for many of the residents' comforts, favored trips to Corbett's Glen in Brighton and Summerville by Lake Ontario.

The Outing, by Sarah Braer, handmade paper, is from the Jewish Home art collection.

A Woman's Touch

It was also in the Depression years (1933) that the Ladies Auxiliary was formed with 125 members, gradually replacing The Daughters Club. Its first president was Hattie Neisner, who held the office until 1940. The treasurer was Rae Edelstein (known for her distinctive hats and colorful reports), a post she occupied until 1958. They were assisted by many remarkable women, including Helen Grossman, Hannah Goldstein, Rose Packer, Julia Rosenberg (who volunteered into the 1980s until she became a resident), and Rebecca Kahn. They worked to take care of the residents' immediate needs—linens, gowns, medical supplies and equipment for the new infirmary. From the first years there were parties given for the residents on Purim, Hanukkah, Passover and Thanksgiving. By 1937, Mrs. Max Gordon, the mother of present board member Burton Gordon, and her committee saw to it that residents were taken on regular weekly excursions during the summer to local parks and to Lake Ontario.

The Home did not step back from its mission during these years. The compassion it showed to those in need—to people like a young Mike Silver, a future president of the Home (1974-76), who came before the Board to plead the case for his chronically ill aunt who could no longer be assisted at home—would make an indelible impression.

The Home was well on its way to fulfilling the goal articulated by Lester Nusbaum when he told the Board: "This home has done a great deal to remove the terror of old age, prevent the separation of old couples, and remove the stigma of pauperism. It has made it possible for these old people to feel that this is their home. We have followed along the lines laid down by the founders. . . . that it should be a real Home in every way. . . ." It was that Jewish spirit of caring that permeated the Home and was exemplified in the dedicated service of the lay supporters, who often passed on their commitment to their children—"from generation to generation."

1928 continued
Rabbi and Mrs. Goldman become superintendent and matron of the Home.

Yeshiva College opens in New York City with Bernard Revel as its head.

1929
The stock market crashes, and a great depression grips the country.

Lilac Sunday becomes Lilac Week, and people from 20 states visit Highland Park.

Forty-five residents are in the Home, including 23 women and 22 men. Seventeen are paying residents, 28 are not.

Patients with little money begin to make the Home sole beneficiary of life insurance plans as compensation for care.

Nurses' call bells are installed in all the rooms.

The Home's Board reprimands a resident for bootlegging.

NBC radio starts broadcasting *The Goldbergs* starring Gertrude Berg.

1930s
The average work week is 45 hours, compared with 60 hours in 1880. U.S. census gives Rochester 328,122 inhabitants, and the county 423,881.

Only 18 states provide any form of aid to the needy aged.

Several books seeking to create a more positive image of the aged in America become bestsellers, among them Elmer Ferris's *Who Says Old?* (1933) and Lyman Powell's *The Second Seventy* (1937).

Making a Home

The Solicitude for the Under-privileged, the Attention Paid to the Aged and Infirm Constitute a Practical Realization of the Jewish Concept of Righteousness. Give to Build a New Infirmary.

The Jewish Home for the Aged . . . all that the name implies . . . was established in 1920 as a Home for the aged and infirm. Steadfast to the ideals which motivated the founders who conceived the thought of providing a safe haven for the aged, the Home has occupied a laudable position in the community service of Rochester. But its service is now being established on a broader base. The infirm, the chronically ill, the senile and blind impose a greater challenge and responsibility. This challenge must be met . . . this responsibility is ours.

The Board fought discouragement over growing deficits during the Depression years and growing waiting lists of needy people.

Cramped conditions and fire hazards made a new infirmary and a corresponding capital campaign a top priority.

The Proposed Infirmary . . . which $45,000 will build

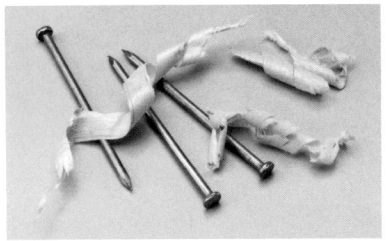

The Depression had hit the Jewish Home hard as supporters suffered their own losses. But as soon as the economy picked up, in the mid-1930s, contributors provided $45,000 quickly and enthusiastically. By 1936, the Jewish Home was again in the headlines.

I remember

Dr. Jacob Kominz always pushed in Board meetings for the Home to accept the most seriously ill applicants—regardless of the high cost of caring for them. His daughter, Esther Friedman, says her father thought about his own family's experience when he saw an elderly man or woman facing a lonely death in the County Home.

"He grew up in poverty, so he had compassion for others," Ms. Friedman says. "His father was ill with asthma and couldn't work. His parents tried opening a confectioner's shop in Rochester, then a grocery business. These were not successful, and they had eight children to support. My father knew from personal experience that some families would have trouble paying."

As a boy, Dr. Kominz sold newspapers in downtown Rochester in front of Ettenheimer's Jewelry Store during the 1880s, making some extra money when sales picked up during the Spanish American War. He sold fireworks in the summer, successfully enough to help pay his way through the University of Rochester and Columbia Medical School. Meanwhile, he did what he could to help his mother and siblings after his father's death.

At the same time he started his family and built a thriving practice, he contributed both hours and passion to high-quality medical care at the Jewish Home.

"Taking care of people," says Ms. Friedman, an active volunteer, was "something that was in the family. My father set an example."

1930s continued

Anti-Semitism rises. Catholic priest Father Charles E. Coughlin charges Jews with "being a part of a conspiracy to dominate Christians everywhere in the world." Radio facilitated the spread of such ideas as speakers reached thousands at once.

The Depression leaves many thousands of Jews unemployed. Many great Jewish philanthropists lose fortunes, or at least some of their ability to donate to charities. Many charitable organizations falter, and overseas aid programs all but disappear.

1930

The Home dedicates the Horace J. Wolf Infirmary in honor of former rabbi of Temple B'rith Kodesh. An article about the dedication cites the Home's service to the indigent as well as its new infirmary, which extends care to disabled elderly beyond most homes for the aged.
Rochester Evening Journal and Post Express, February 24, 1930

The medical staff at the Home mourns the death of Dr. Nathan W. Soble, who served on a committee of three as the Board of Censors for the Home. A resolution in his honor said, "He gave of himself freely and unstintingly for the relief of suffering humanity....Many a human being was transformed into another personality by contact with him." Minutes from Annual Meeting of Medical Staff, 1923-1953

A membership campaign begins with the goal of 1,000 new members for the Home.

Garson Grossman becomes the first hired "general field secretary."

A grievance committee forms to "straighten out the little differences between the folks in the Home."

1931

Rochester wins national health award.

When Jewish hospital patients in Rochester have no relatives, Jewish Social Service provides kosher food.

The Home gives help and advice to newer institutions, including the New Haven, Conn., Home for the Aged and the Des Moines, Iowa, Home for the Aged.

A library begins at the Home, and Jewish books are accepted for donation.

1932

The Community Chest raises $1,107,377, but is short almost a quarter of a million dollars.

The Board orders that "a temporary reduction of 10% be made in all wages and salaries to meet a reduction of the budget as notified to us by the Community Chest. All salaries will be replaced when the emergency passes."

The Budget Committee approves a deficit of $879.88 for the year. Nurses are not allowed time off. The Minutes note: "Amount will have to come from their salaries if they wish time off."

The Council of Jewish Federations and Welfare Funds is organized to give organizational expenses to Jewish philanthropy.

The Home installs a coin box telephone to save on telephone charges.

"Temporary elimination of night watchman. All food weighed. Complete inventory of all linens, silver, and supplies in the Home....No meals [are to] be served in the Home to transients, [but instead] prepared and given to the person to eat out of the building."
Minutes, 1930-1933

1933

President Roosevelt orders all banks closed for 4 days.

The U.S. government repeals Prohibition.

Rochester's clothing industry employs 7,500, produces $32 million in goods, and pays workers $12 million despite Depression.

"Reported that 34 old folks contributed to the Community Chest from their spending money—a total of $20.75." U.S. unemployment is estimated to be 13 million.

The Ladies Auxiliary is established.

Adolf Hitler becomes chancellor of Germany in January. On May 10, the Nazis hold a public burning of books by Jewish authors.

A national boycott of German goods is organized and the Jewish Home physicians participate.

The Home purchases an American and a Zionist flag from Rochester Stationery Co.

Jewish businesses around the Home thrived, and residents enjoyed the fruits of their success. Nearly every photograph from the Home's early years shows a resident enjoying some gift—eating hard candy from Neisner's Department store, drinking a bottle of 7-Up from Goldstein's Bottleworks, reading a copy of Henry Weis's donation of The Day.

Board member Frank Sherman secured fresh fruit and vegetables from the Public Market, which he gave to the Home. In 1929, he donated 82 bushels of potatoes, 12 bushels of onions, and a bushel of turnips along with 700 pounds of grapes (valued at $35) that he helped transform into 50 gallons of wine, despite Prohibition.

Public Market,
*above, is an oil
painting by
Brian Shapiro
on display
at the Home.*

*"Many Jewish people
made their own wine for
religious purposes during
these years," recalls Dr.
David Eisenberg, a long-
time volunteer on the
Home's medical staff.
"There was no reliable source for
kosher wine."*

*After hearing the discussion
of Frank Sherman's donations
during a board meeting, Dr.
Kominz commented, "The old
members were never as happy as
they are now."*

1934
A conference of all
shuls and Jewish soci-
eties in western New
York meets at Beth
Hamedresh Hagadol,
Hanover Street. A
committee of five
represents the Home.
Minutes, 1934-1942

The Home's deficit
rises to $2,000.

According to the
Minutes, the fire
marshal states that the
Home "has used up
five times the area
allowed according to
the new code for frame
buildings. It is a viola-
tion of the law to keep
employees on the third
floor. The law does not
allow institutions built
of wood. Suggested
a fireproof wall to cut
off the remodeled
building, fire escapes
and tube."

The Department of
Public Welfare recom-
mends admission of a
couple as soon as
room is available, and
offers to pay $4.00
each per week for their
care and the cost of
medicine.

Plans are approved to
"go ahead with the
building of the much
needed addition."

"This home has done a great deal to remove the terror of old age, prevent the separation of old couples, and remove the stigma of pauperism. It has made it possible for these old people to feel that this is their home."

Lester Nusbaum, 9th Annual Meeting, January 19, 1926

chapter two

The War and Modern Care

"Honoring parents
means that a child must supply
his parents with food and drink,
provide them with clothes
and footwear, and assist their
coming in and going out
of their home."

Talmud Kiddushin

1935 - 1949

The 1945 fundraising brochure at right helped raise money to complete a million-dollar building for the Jewish Home.

Conditions were cramped at the Home throughout the war years, but residents continued to enjoy such pleasures as reading the Yiddish newspaper and petting a cat in the sunroom.

"*The Home is one of the few places on earth where need, not influence, opens doors.*"

Jewish Home fund-raising brochure, January 1945

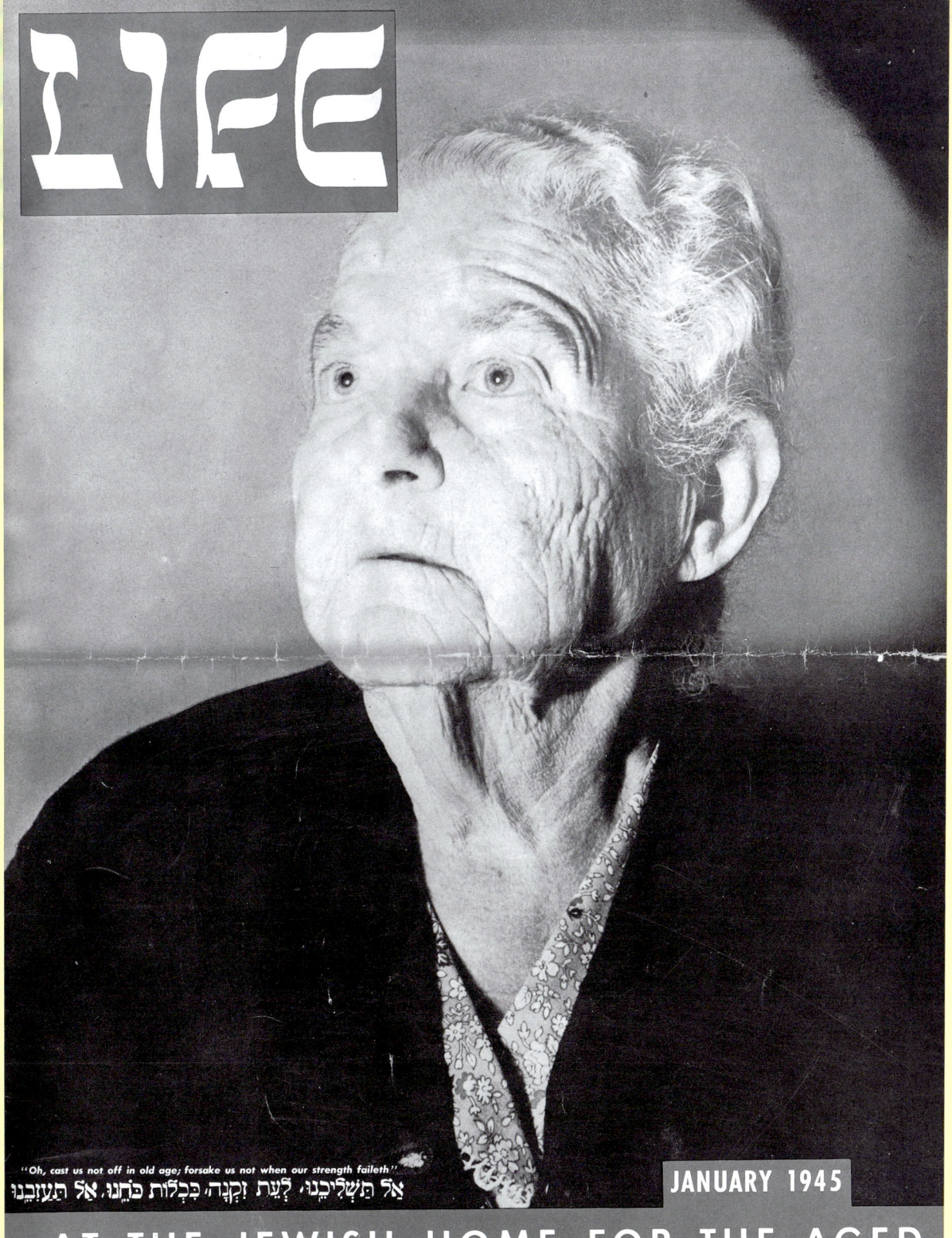

LIFE

"Oh, cast us not off in old age; forsake us not when our strength faileth".

אַל תַּשְׁלִיכֵנוּ לְעֵת זִקְנָה, כִּכְלוֹת כֹּחֵנוּ, אַל תַּעַזְבֵנוּ

JANUARY 1945

AT THE JEWISH HOME FOR THE AGED
1162 ST. PAUL STREET ★ ROCHESTER 5, NEW YORK

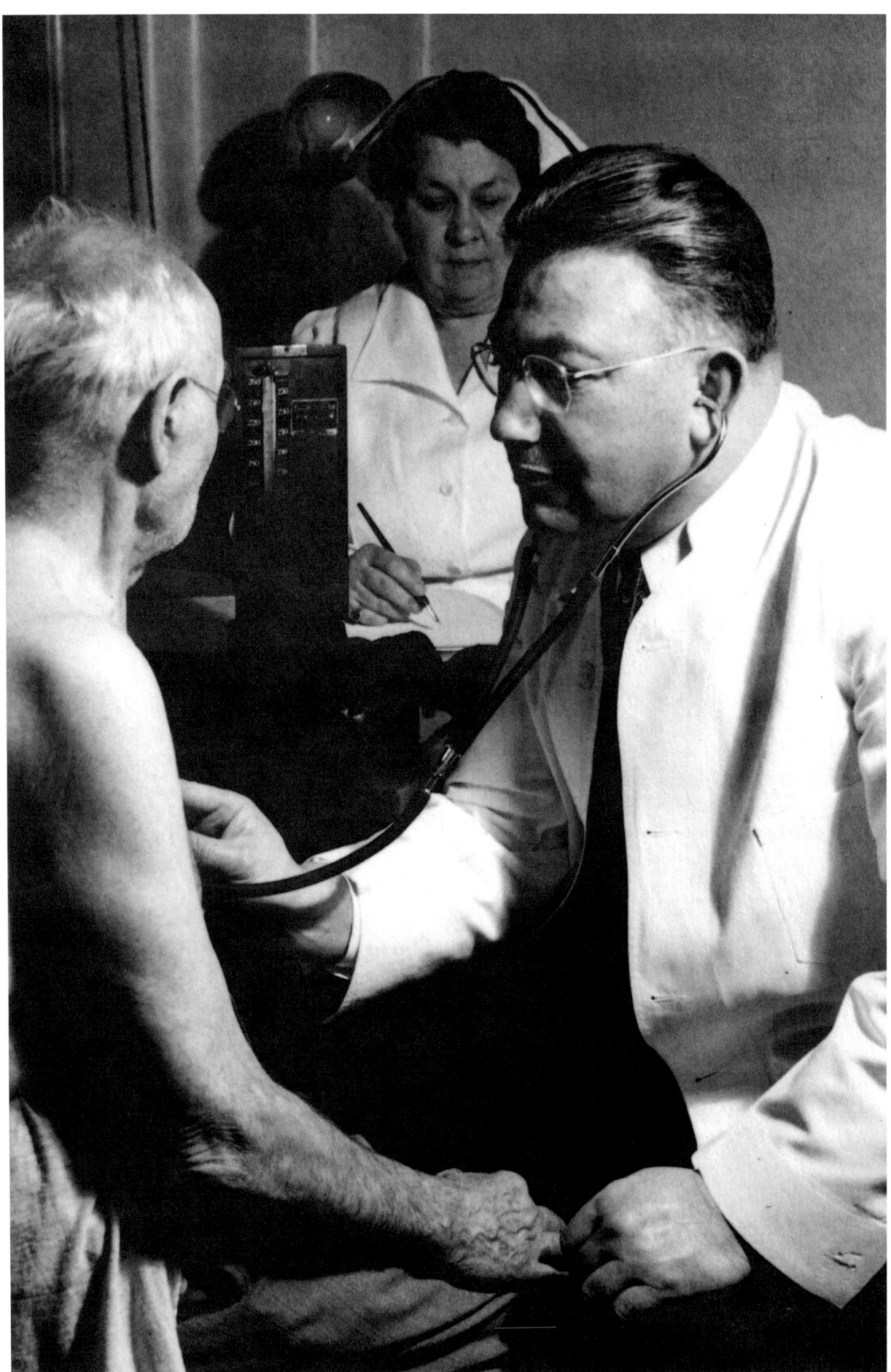

The Roosevelt New Deal

The Social Security Act, enacted on August 14, 1935, softened the hardships incurred by individuals and institutions alike by providing an annual guaranteed income for the elderly on which homes for the aging could depend for basic income. Supplemental financial sources, including Community Chest monies, private donations, residents' fees, and private and public health insurance payments gradually allowed enhancement of the services rendered and the overall quality of Jewish homes for the aged. Here again, the Rochester Jewish Home for the Aged and Infirm Aged was recognized as a leader in providing services and innovative programming.

By 1937, there were 67 residents in the Home, 27 men and 40 women. Most were born in Eastern Europe and Yiddish was their native language. This was to some degree still true of the Board as well. Therefore, minutes of the Board meetings of the Home, taken by Belle Fenig until her retirement in 1948, were alternately recorded in Yiddish and English.

At left, Dr. William S. Ruben is shown examining a patient.

Jewish doctors in the Rochester community supported the Jewish Home from the beginning. As medicine became more specialized in the 1940s, many more doctors offered their services. According to the Old Folks *newsletter, "the resident physician has at his call a competent staff of medical specialists."*

These included three surgeons, three cardiologists, two gastroenterologists, three allergists, three dermatologists, four psychiatrists, two orthopedic surgeons, two specialists in rheumatic diseases, four gynecologists, one ear, nose and throat specialist, one ophthalmologist and two urologists."

I Remember

Ruben Dankoff, a lawyer and past president of the Jewish Home Board, came up with the idea for a fund-raising brochure that imitated the style of *Life* magazine. "My daughter's grandmother, Mrs. Naditz, made the cover," he recalls. "It was a successful solicitation, and nobody sued us for copyright infringement."

During the next few years, as the number of elderly Jews in Rochester increased and the Home became known for its high quality of care, the list of applicants escalated. The median age of the residents was 62 (today it is 87), and many were seriously ill and in need of infirmary care.

"Residents fill the Home to capacity," Superintendent Sam Krawetz told the Board at a meeting in 1938. "Even the solarium holds patients, and many more elderly urgently need care." The Board even discussed the advisability of asking the county to establish a kosher kitchen in the county hospital because the Home was filled to capacity. These demands placed new pressures on the Board to make prudent choices in deciding which applicants to accept. While need was still the defining criterion, those with ailments the Home could not treat were referred to area hospitals. But determining who was the most needy required, as one leader commented, "the wisdom of Solomon."

Meanwhile, the community continued to pitch in with contributions of all sorts. The Neisner family donated 24 gallons of ice cream in one year. Sidney and Abraham Grossman of Dollar Dry Cleaning Company cleaned 450 drapes and pieces of clothing. Morris Rosenbloom, the grandfather of future leader Bob Weinberg, provided fresh fruits and vegetables from his farm in Pittsford.

Need for the Home's services grew dramatically in 1930s. The 1937 fireproof wing, shown below, filled to capacity within just one year after its dedication.

A group of Rochester dentists, including Drs. Maurice Dankoff, Benjamin Keyfetz, George Joel, Wolf Lasker, Garson Rosenthal, and Michael Kowal, began providing free dental care to residents. Other supporters made provisions in their wills to leave generous bequests to the Home. Many made gifts in memory of deceased family members or bar-mitzvahed youngsters.

As the Depression finally lifted, stipends from New York State and the federal government flowed in under the aegis of various welfare programs targeted specifically for needy elderly people. Even though the Home still required more space, it was relatively solvent, managing to pay off all its debts and its mortgage. It could afford what were perceived as luxuries at the time—dentures for needy residents, an oxygen tank, a part-time resident attending physician, and a carefully developed publicity program aimed at soliciting community support and donations.

The Gathering Storm

But devastating reports about the growth of Nazism and Hitler's menacing grip on Europe began to dilute the brief euphoria set off by the country's recovering economy. Discussions concerning boycotting German goods began to circulate. Drs. Isadore Messinger and David Wolin urged their colleagues not to use German drugs.

1935

The Social Security Act of 1935 gives older people the income security needed to live with relatives or with foster families. To receive Social Security, it was stipulated, one could not live in the poorhouses in which so many elderly were trapped. The government hoped to send the formerly destitute elderly into families, but instead saw the number of for-profit boardinghouses grow. Eventually, these houses added medical staffs and were designated "nursing homes."

Sixty-eight residents are in the Home—42 women and 26 men.

Certain elderly receive full-time day care, but "sleep out" because of the Home's shortage of beds.

Lester Nusbaum appoints a committee to visit every synagogue during the high holidays and present the Home's financial needs.

The roof badly needs repairs.

Franklin D. Roosevelt makes a campaign speech in Rochester.

Almost every American is issued a Social Security Number.

Plans for the addition include an "up-to-date equipped laundry," "a mortuary to prepare the deceased for burial," and a "chapel for funeral services which will seat about 104 people. Everything for the comfort, convenience and safety of these old folks has been taken into consideration. This building will be 100% fire-proof."

The Home becomes a voting member at the National Convention of Jewish Social Service.

Relief costs Rochester and Monroe County more than $8 million.

Jews in the Home suffered as they listened intensely to reports on the radio and wondered whether their families and friends, many stranded in Germany, Poland and other Eastern European countries, would survive the coming Holocaust. The Home also began receiving requests to shelter Jews desperately seeking ways to escape.

The plight of the Jews in Europe presented an urgent challenge. Rabbis Philip Bernstein, of Temple B'rith Kodesh, and Henry Fisher, of Temple Beth El, called repeatedly for official American protestations against Hitler's violence. As fugitives from Germany and Austria reached Rochester during the late 1930s, local Jewish leaders formed the Rochester Refugee Service to assist them in finding homes and jobs. Approximately 700 refugees were settled in the city during the 1930s and early 1940s. The Home employed several of them, including a physician, Dr. Harry Rothschild.

One of those stranded overseas was Rabbi Martin Solomonsky, a renowned religious leader in Germany. His daughter and son-in-law, Dr and Mrs. Herzog, lived in Rochester. Rabbi Solomonsky had already been in several concentration camps by 1939 and his daughter feared that if he depended on routine exit

policies, he would never be able to leave Europe. She asked Rabbi Bernstein to help. Rabbi Bernstein was already making his mark as a leader in the Reform movement and would eventually become instrumental in the resettlement of refugees after the war. He persuaded the Board to offer Rabbi Solomonsky a job as religious director of the Home, hoping that the invitation would expedite his departure from Germany. The authorities honored the request and Rabbi Solomonsky moved to Rochester, becoming director of religious programs for two years.

Other Jews were not so lucky. As press reports about their dire fate and the growing power of Hitler continued, the spirits of those in the Home plummeted. When the United States finally sent troops to Europe in 1941, residents tried to help out by writing letters to loved ones and knitting scarves for soldiers. Meanwhile, they stoically endured the cutbacks and restrictions imposed by the war. Many personnel left to fight overseas. Food costs rose and rationing began. Because of the war work and gas rationing, the number of Board meetings was drastically reduced. There was heated debate over whether to cut costs even further by limiting

chicken dinners—a Friday night delicacy—to once every other week. (Eventually, the Home did so, saving $1,000 a year.) The shortage of space became more acute. There was no room set aside for dying residents, no isolation rooms for the critically ill or mentally impaired and limited supplies of clothing, medicine and other basic supplies.

To cope with some of the space problems, in 1942 the Home purchased a house on Avenue A to provide room for employees, so that the Home could accommodate more residents. (Soon, the number of residents rose to 83.) Even though the building campaign was put on hold through the war years, donations continued. When Hattie Neisner's husband, Joseph, died, his employees raised $10,000 for the Building Fund as a memorial.

The End of an Era

July 13, 1943, would be the last meeting of the Board that Lester Nusbaum would officiate as president. He gave an eloquent valedictory, recounting the progress made from modest beginnings to an established institution with assets of approximately $200,000, with no debts and no mortgages. He reminded the Board "that kindness in consideration of the old folks is imperative," and he urged them to conduct the Home

With the medical advancements of the twentieth century—from x-ray machines to recreational therapy—came not only higher expectations for health but a steeper price tag for medical care. The Home became more than a place to rest quietly—but one that, in its words, offered to "add life to years."

1936

A groundbreaking ceremony for the new infirmary takes place on May 26, with Mr. Nusbaum turning the first shovel of dirt.

Mr. Samuel Krawetz becomes a religious director of the Home and applies to the railroad for a reverend's pass.

A memorial resolution honoring Alfred Hart, a trustee of the Home, states: "The measure of one's true value to a community depends upon his importance to its philanthropic, charitable, and social agencies."

The Rabbinical Council of America, composed of English-speaking Orthodox rabbis, is organized in 1935.

The Central Conference of American Rabbis (Reform) adopts the resolution that Zionism is "a matter of personal conscience."

Adolf Hitler consolidates his power in Germany.

Nazi Germany adopts the Nuremberg laws in 1935. This action officially disenfranchises Jews and classifies them as noncitizens.

1937

The Home's new infirmary opens.

The Ladies Auxiliary now provides all the necessary medical equipment, furnishings, and linens for the new infirmary.

Some residents receive Old Age Assistance to help pay for their care at the Home.

Residents pay between $10 and $25 a week, depending upon their financial resources. The average cost per resident is $10.43 a week.

48

The War and Modern Care

according to traditional laws and customs and in the spirit of Jewish caring. He expressed thanks to all who assisted, particularly the doctors for their advice and services given free of charge. A chapter was closed with his retirement, but the mantle of leadership was transferred to able hands with links to the past, and access to the challenges and opportunities of the future.

Changing of the Guard

On July 25, 1943, Garson Meyer, the son of founding member Sarah Meyer, was elected president. Meyer, a chief chemist at Kodak, eventually earned the title "Mr. Aging" for his devotion to the Home and other organizations committed to refining the quality of life for the elderly. "He was a gentle, sensitive, committed person," recalled William Greenberg, the administrator of the Home from 1957 to 1984. "He saw older people as people. And he believed they needed care in a setting that enabled them to develop their abilities with dignity and respect. Sarah [Meyer] epitomized the type of person who was concerned about the needs of others. Garson got his sensitivity from this background." With Meyer came some other outstanding leaders, men with vision and courage, who were instrumental in positioning the Home for major initiatives of modernization and innovation—people like Ruben A. Dankoff (chair of the Admissions Committee), Samuel Greenhouse (chair of the

Although belts continued to tighten during the war years, traditional but increasingly expensive chicken dinners remained a priority for residents.

Finance Committee and Fund Raising), Harry Germanow (responsible for membership), and Dr. Eli A. Leven (chair of the Medical Committee and head physician at the Home).

The news clipping at right records the story of Benjamin Epstein, a 103-year-old resident, who received a misdirected telegram ordering him to report for active service.

This Veteran Is Draft-Proof

ROCHESTER, N. Y., Oct. 29 (AP) —There was a telegram from the Department of Defense yesterday for Benjamin Epstein ordering him to report for active military duty with the United States Army. Ben Epstein, whose last stint of active duty was with the army of the Czar of Russia around 1871, was puzzled. Orderlies at the Rochester Jewish Home for the Aged returned the telegram to Western Union. It could not be for their Ben, for he is 103 years old.

In May 1946, Samuel Krawetz resigned as superintendent after fourteen years of service, because of poor health. The Board thanked this gentle man, who "has drunk deeply at the springs of Jewish religious and ethical living. . . . He has worked physically to preserve the bodies of our aged and infirm. But more than that, he has given, without stint or reservation, of his knowledge, of his faith, of his . . . fervor, of his humane understanding."

Digging New Roots

When the war finally ended, in 1945, spirits rose and the Board decided to move forward with its campaign to finance a new building. It also brought in professionals who would modernize and streamline the efficiency of the Home. In September 1946, it hired Eli Rudin as its first executive director. Rudin, trained as a social worker, had worked as a director of the USO in South Dakota and director of adult activities at the Rochester JYMWA (Jewish Young Men's and Women's Association), the predecessor of the Jewish Community Center. "Sam Greenhouse and Garson Meyer wanted some professional help," recalled Rudin. "And they needed help. When we went to the library to find books on geriatrics, all we

found was one book, on the potential of Social Security. We really had to start from scratch!"

Eli Rudin and Garson Meyer helped bring the Home into the modern age. Together they ventured into new territory, learning along the way by experiment and resourcefulness, until they became

A young Barbara Dankoff Bolton, daughter of then board member Reuben Dankoff, sits with her grandmother, Mrs. Naditz.

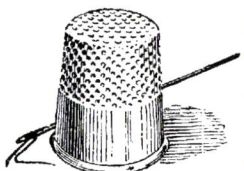

"We certainly knew that the war was officially over when Mrs. Morris Schlossman and her sewing committee came back to turn the raw material of cloth and thread into beautiful drapes, towels, sheets, aprons."

Old Folks, September 1947

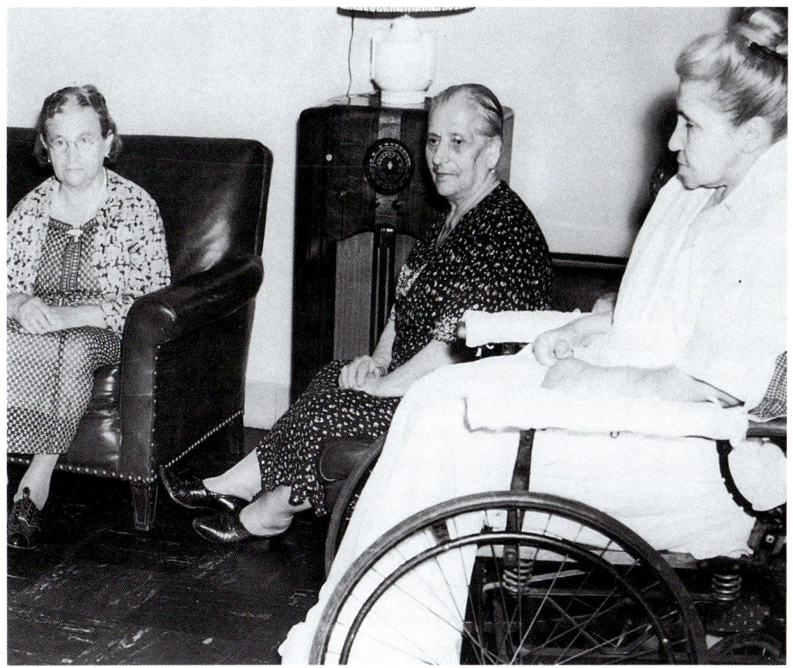

Residents listened to the events of WW II on the radio, knitting scarves for soldiers and hoping for the end of a war that took away beloved family members and volunteers.

Overcrowding at the Home left little elbow room for residents in the dining room during a Passover seder.

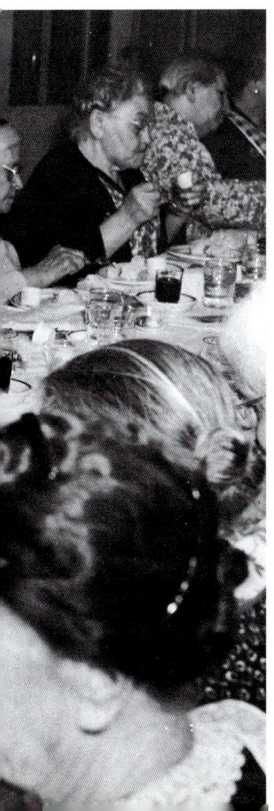

1938 continued
The Home's waiting list grows. Most new applications are infirmary cases.

At the Eighteenth Annual Dinner Dance for the Jewish Home for the Aged and Aged Infirm held at the Seneca Hotel, the Home is called "A great humane Institution dedicated to the relief of human suffering."

Kristallnacht (Night of the Broken Glass) riots occur in Germany.

1939
Brina Appelbaum, a founder of the Home, becomes a resident. She tells the Board she is "now a permanent guest of the Home and is happy."

Mr. Krawetz reports to the Board, "While it is not difficult to keep the women residents in clothes, the matter of clothing for the men is a problem."

The Home completes its 18th year with practically no debts. Jewish Children's Home in Rochester celebrates its 25th anniversary.

Nazi Germany institutes a euthanasia program in which "persons who, according to human judgment, are incurably ill may, upon the most serious evaluation of their medical condition, be accorded a mercy death." The Nazis began by killing the elderly and infirm members of non-Aryan ethnic groups.

For every 100 families in Rochester, there are 100 radios and 93 automobiles. A new traffic code allows 35 m.p.h. on arterial highways. Britain issues a White Paper limiting Jewish emigration to Palestine to 75,000 over the next five years.

Germany invades Poland, initiating World War II.

1940
9,019,314 Americans, or 6.8 percent of the population, are 65 and older; 36.5 percent are 45 and older.

Doctors create five classifications for residents —aged, infirm, active chronics, stationary chronics, and blind.

The Nazis begin construction of a wall to enclose the future Warsaw ghetto.

Until the 1940s, official notes at the Home were alternately taken in Yiddish and English.

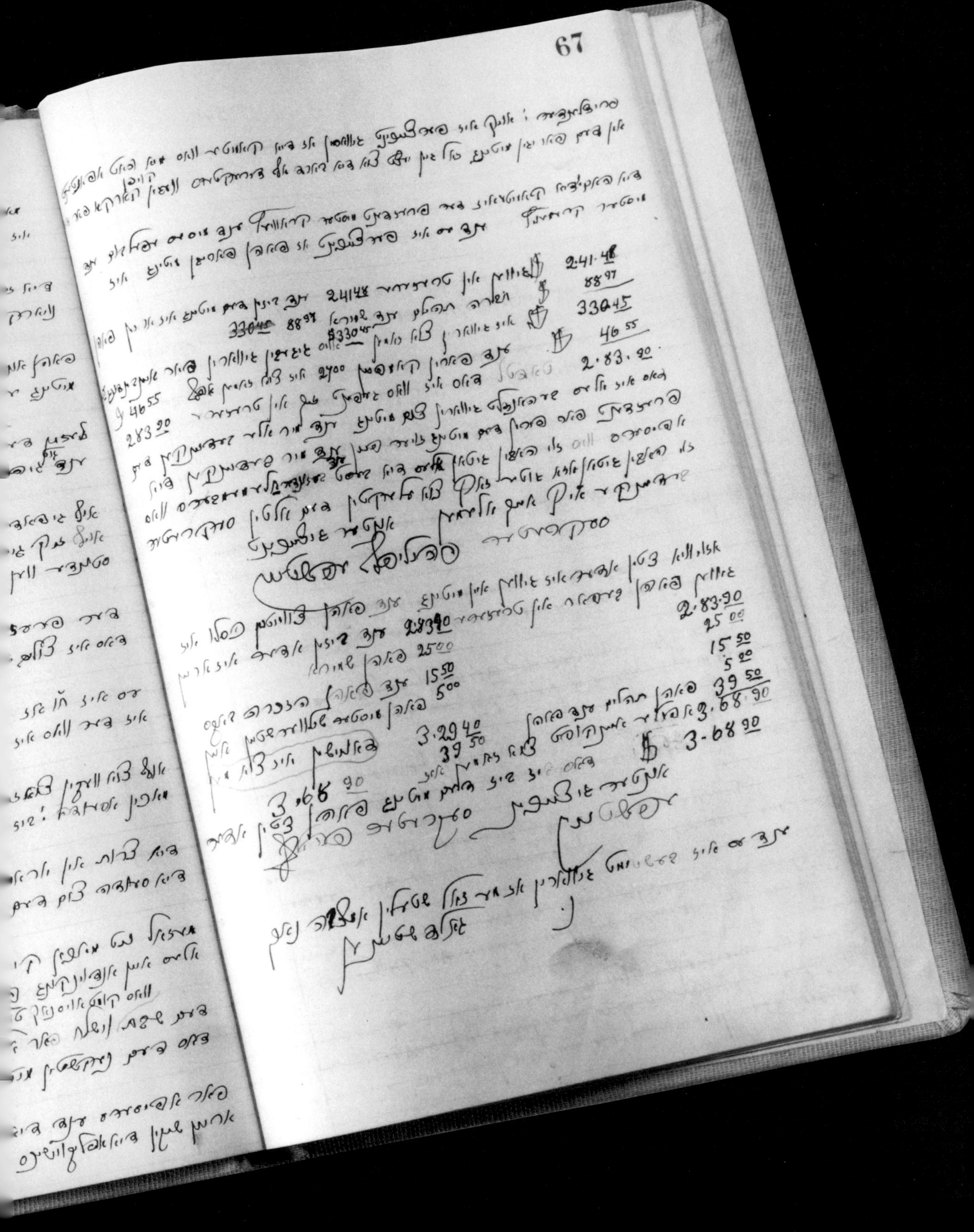

2.41.48
88.97
330.45
$330.45
46.55
2.83.90
283.90
2700

2.83.90
25.00
15.50
5.00
39.50
3.68.90
3.29.40
3.68.90
$3.68.90

experts in the care of the aged. The field was becoming more professionalized, and they, on the local level first and then nationally, had a great deal to do with furthering the process.

One of the Home's first needs was to improve the facility. The Board initiated a capital campaign to raise $1 million, not only to build a new structure but to expand its medical facilities, recreational programs, social services and religious services. Joe Silverstein and M. Harry Goldman were appointed to spearhead the effort. "The residents had no money," Eli Rudin reflected. "The Home had no endowments and no resources. The Board had guts and were willing to gamble." The characteristics of courage

and foresight have always been a trademark of the leadership of the Home.

Part of the Board's strategy involved seeking out new members who would contribute expertise and solidify the Home's connections with the growing business community. These new directors included Morris Manson, of the Manson News Agency, Dr. Michael Kowal, a local dentist, M. Harry Goldman of Neisner Brothers, and Sam Appelbaum of Tapetex Products. Morris Manson later left a major bequest to the Home in 1987. Even so, getting money turned out to be an uphill battle. Despite the impressive array of businessmen on the Board, no Rochester bank would

underwrite a mortgage for a nonprofit, single-purpose building.

Finally, Board members heard about a bank in Buffalo, the Erie County Savings Bank, that had recently financed a hospital. Led by Ruben Dankoff and Ladies Auxiliary president Florence Rubens, a group traveled there to meet with bank officers. After thirteen Board members put their own assets at risk, the bank agreed to finance a loan for $250,000, an act that suddenly made many banks in Rochester eager to receive the Home's business.

The Board, however, still needed more money, and it turned to the community. The Ladies Auxiliary held major fund-raising events and the Home mailed thousands of solicitations regularly to prospective donors. This was happening as the Jewish community in Rochester was itself beginning to change socially, economically and religiously. In the early decades of the twentieth century, the manufacture of men's clothing was one of Rochester's major industries. Both employees and employers were largely Jewish, as was true in other major cities. But by the early 1950s, Rochester's share in the national output of men's clothing was modest. Four large firms, outgrowths of earlier mergers—Michaels Stern, Hickey-Freeman,

Statistics and needs for the Home taken from a 1943 report to the Community Chest seem impossible by today's standards:

Statistics:
77 Residents
3 Day Boarders
Staff 26

Needs:
Present Infirmary Difficulties.
Lack of space.
No emergency room for dying residents.
No isolation room.
Food must be brought from kitchen.
Only 2 bathrooms to accommodate 27 occupants, besides nurses and doctors.

I Remember

A reporter for the *Democrat and Chronicle* (April 9, 1952) once followed around the Home's president, Garson Meyer, and his 92-year-old mother, Sarah, one of its founders.

"I rarely heard her speak," Pat Barry recalled, "except for a few Hebrew words of greeting this one or that one of the oldsters who clamored for her attention. 'Please,' begged an eager person, 'come for seder with us.'

"'I must, Mrs. Meyer, have two hours to talk with you,' announced another spectacled woman."

The reporter called Mrs. Meyer a gifted listener and an inspiration for her son, who took up her cause for the Home, serving as president between 1943 and 1952. Side by side, Garson and Sarah dedicated the cornerstone of the new Home.

William Greenberg, administrator of the Home from 1957 to 1984, remembers Garson Meyer as a "gentle, sensitive, committed person" who gained national recognition for his leadership as an advocate for the elderly "long before it was popular. He saw older people as people. And he believed they needed care in a setting which enabled them to develop their abilities with dignity and respect. Sarah epitomized the type of person who was concerned about the needs of others. Garson got his sensitivity from this background."

The Home finally broke ground for the new building in 1948. The fund-raising campaign, headed by Joseph Silverstein and M. Harry Goldman, was at that time working toward what seemed an impossible goal of $500,000.

Discussing plans for the new building in 1948 are Joseph Silverstein, architect Ben Ade, Garson Meyer, and Eli Rudin.

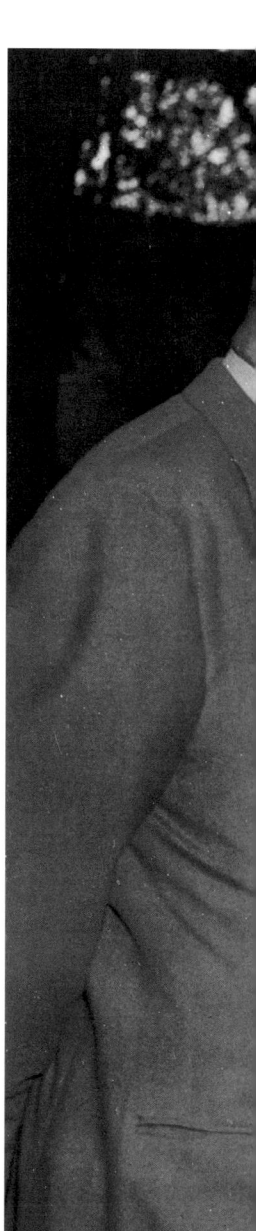

Fashion Park and Timely Clothes—continued to serve the finer men's clothing market. Bond Stores was expanding its production facilities, but basically the industry had seen better days. Only one clothing factory, Hickey-Freeman Co., remains today.

The children of these immigrant workers pursued secular education and careers and for the most part moved out of the working class into the professions and business. Their high educational level led to considerable increases in income. The move from city to suburbs, which began at the end of the war, accelerated. As they married, they moved away from the Joseph Avenue neighborhood. Many bought homes in the Monroe Avenue area and joined the conservative congregation Temple Beth El or the Reform congregation Temple B'rith Kodesh. Both of these synagogues enjoyed significant increases in membership in the postwar decades. Others moved to the contiguous suburbs of Brighton and

The sign, below, stood in front of the Jewish Home's construction site and reiterated its mission to "add life to years."

The War and Modern Care

Irondequoit. In 1950, approximately 75 percent of Greater Rochester's Jews lived in the city. In 1960, that number declined to 63 percent; in 1980, it was only 24 percent and in 1990 it was less than 15 percent.

The community was changing demographically to a largely American-born, suburban community of salaried professionals and business people whose religious affiliation remained steady but transforming and whose lives were less and less directed by religious disciplines. They were comfortable in their dual identity as Americans and as Jews. It was the energy, competence and professionalism of this new postwar generation that was to propel the Home forward in the next decades—a progress influenced by a deep, instinctive commitment to the values of the past, but with a view toward the requirements of the future.

While most of the residents of the Home continued to be observant Jews born in Europe, many of their children no longer subscribed as strictly to these traditional ways. They began to affiliate with the other denominations of Judaism, and their level of observance of ritual began to fall off. For example, many drove on Saturdays and were less meticulous in their practice of the laws of *kashrut*. The number of kosher butchers has declined from ten in the 1940s to one, Lipman's Kosher Market, in the 1990s. However, they still recognized the importance that this religious orientation had for the residents of the Home, then and for the future, and were committed to maintaining allegiance to that ethos.

This new generation of largely American-born and secularly educated Jews became active in the Home as Board members, volunteers and donors. They infused the Home with new ideas, programs and contributions of all sorts, while preserving the value of what was already there. Dorothy Burns, a member of the Ladies Auxiliary, began an intensive program of recreation and occupational therapy for residents. The Memorial Art Gallery provided a new type of loom for weaving mufflers and afghans. Sylvia Rothschild, an adult worker at the JYMWA, organized workshops where residents could make Hanukkah presents for their grandchildren. In other workshops residents made colorful potholders, aprons and note collectors—some of which they actually sold to raise small amounts of money. A library was eventually set up and educational programs, including classes in the English language, were instituted. Outings continued to places as diverse as the Shrine Circus, the Irondequoit Country Club and the Idlers Club on Beach Avenue facing Lake Ontario.

When television appeared in the late 1940s, the Home was one of the first institutions to receive a set, a gift from a generous supporter. The new invention did almost as much to reform the lives of residents as the automobile, bringing them into daily contact with everything from daily news reports to the antics of Uncle Miltie and the eclectic entertainment of the *Ed Sullivan Show*. While tele-

continued on page 62

The Board appoints three representatives of the medical staff to the Board: Dr. Eli Leven, Dr. Curt Falkenheim, and Dr. Saul Moress.

A conference of Nazi officials is held at Wannsee to discuss the implementation of the "final solution of the Jewish question."

1943
Basic membership at the Home is still $6 a year.

The government authorizes Home superintendent Samuel Krawetz and Belle Fenig, executive secretary, to sign ration checks and endorse ration certificates.

The Home has assets of approximately $200,000, with no debts and no mortgages.

The Home purchases a house with several apartments on 41-43 Avenue A to provide housing for employees and give more space to residents at the Home.

Mordecai Anielewicz leads the first armed resistance in the Warsaw ghetto.

1944
Brina Appelbaum, one of the Home's founders, dies at the Home. The Board expresses its gratitude for her work, noting:

"In the fashion characteristic of the best in Jewish Womanhood she gave of her wealth, her time, her thought, to the Home's development."

The building fund rises to approximately $200,000.

"Only as one's life concerns itself with the problems, the cares, the development and the service of others does one advance spiritually."

Board of the Jewish Home upon the retirement of Superintendent Samuel Krawetz

Residents and supporters together dedicate the new synagogue.

57

The newsletter *Old Folks* records
every phase of construction as the
Home's modern new building took
shape. The project presented special
challenges as the builders had to
accommodate life as usual in the
Home's old buildings, two frame
houses and a brick wing. "Construction on the new Home is in full
swing. The great steam shovels have
gnawed out an impressive hole in
the hillside atop which the present

Home sits. Structural steel is piled
up ready for use, and, perhaps, even
as you read this, the first members
of the huge steel skeleton which will
carry the mass of the new building
will be riveted in place. Now that
the long-awaited day has arrived,
the post-war expansion program
must be backed with dollars pledged
in the past and dollars to be pledged
in the near future."

Old Folks, April 1949

Garson Meyer, Sarah Meyer, Lester Nusbaum, and Rabbi Leon Stitskin were just a few of those present to dedicate the cornerstone of the Home's new building on December 11, 1949.

1944 continued

Mechanics Institute, founded in 1829, adopts a new name—Rochester Institute of Technology.

The United States establishes a "free port" at Oswego, N.Y., for 1,000 refugees from Nazism.

1945

The war makes drugs more difficult to obtain. The Home must file an application with the U.S. Treasury Department and pay a special stamp tax to handle narcotics.

Anne Frank and her sister, Margot, die at Bergen-Belsen.

Harry S. Truman becomes president upon the death of Franklin D. Roosevelt.

Nuclear weapons are dropped on Hiroshima and Nagasaki, Japan.

World War II ends.

1946

Eli H. Rudin becomes executive director of the Home at a salary of $4,000 a year.

Cutting chicken dinners to every other week saves the Home $1,000 a year.

The Home proceeds with plans for a new building but must contend with materials shortages and rising building costs as post-war rebuilding booms across the country.

Sylvia Rothschild, adult worker at the JYMA, organizes a recreational craft program for residents. They begin by making Hanukkah presents for grandchildren.

The King David Hotel in Jerusalem is blown up by an Irgun operation.

1947

The Home has the largest backlog of applicants ever and commits to raising an additional $300,000 for a new building.

Harold Rand, director of public relations for the City of Rochester, begins to edit *Old Folks*, a newspaper for the Home.

Friend of the Home Haskell Marks dies. He is a former member of the New York State Assembly and former city treasurer of Rochester.

The Rochester Jewish Home for the Aged and Aged Infirm celebrates 25 years of successful service to Rochester's Jewish community at a silver anniversary dinner at the Seneca Hotel.

Eli Rudin and Garson Meyer speak on the *Red Feather Program*, a radio show sponsored by the Rochester Community Chest. They discuss both the Home's services and the many community programs for the aged that involve the Inter-Faith Committee of Church Women, oldsters' clubs, club meetings at the Baden Street Settlement, and the Women's Educational and Industrial Union.

61

1947 continued
To meet the needs of Conservative Jewish youth, the Ramah summer camps are founded.

Many new people join the Home's staff—a new director, new bookkeeper, new cook, new matron, new head nurse, and new office worker.

Dorothy Burns, consultant for social agencies, and the Ladies Auxiliary begin a more intensive program of recreation and occupational therapy. The Memorial Art Gallery provides a new type of loom for weaving mufflers and afghans.

The Rochester Savings Bank elects Garson Meyer Citizen of the Day for his work with the Jewish Home and his chairmanship of the Care of the Aged section of the Council of Social Agencies.

The Rochester Shriners transport 30 residents to a complete matinee performance of the Shrine Circus.

Hillel School is established in Rochester as its first Hebrew day school.

Nearly 300 members attend a meeting of the Ladies Auxiliary, held at the Hotel Seneca in October. Sol Linowitz gives a "stirring review" of *Blessed Is the Match*.

Exodus 1947, an immigrant ship bearing 4,550 Jews, is forcibly turned back by the British.

1948
Haloid Co. introduces xerography.

The War and Modern Care

continued from page 56
vision became a favorite recreation from the beginning, the personalities who received the most attention in these early days were neither Walter Cronkite nor Milton Berle, but wrestlers! Soon, wrestling matches became so popular with seniors that Bob Turner, a sportscaster for WHAM-TV, took a moment out of his narrative to send special greetings to fans at the Home.

The New Home

The Home also began to chronicle its activities and daily events, recruiting Harold Rand (the public relations director for the City of Rochester) to edit a newsletter called, appropriately, *Old Folks*. The newsletter not only highlighted the various crafts programs and social events held at the Home, but also diligently recorded the progress of the building fund campaign. This fund finally reached a turning point in 1948, when a combination of individual donations and loans from the bank gave the Board the needed incentive to go ahead with the new building. In June 1948, the Board authorized the architectural firm of Ade & Todd to proceed with the plans for the new building.

According to a report in *Old Folks*, the new home would be "built around an inner court area and set off by sweeping, modern lines. All living quarters would face outside so there is no feeling of being enclosed. . . . The fifth floor will be kept for cases requiring special medical care, such as therapeutic treatments, swirl baths and the like." Ground was broken in 1948 and, as plans progressed, *Old Folks* recorded every phase of construction—a challenge because the builders had to accommodate life as usual in the Home's old buildings, two frame houses and a brick wing, while constructing the new one.

"Construction on the new Home is in full swing," reported *Old Folks* in April 1949. "The great steam shovels have gnawed out an impressive hole in the hillside atop which the present Home sits. Structural steel is piled up ready for use, and, perhaps, even as you read this, the first members of the huge steel skeleton which will carry the mass of the new building will be riveted in place."

The cornerstone for the new building was finally dedicated on December 11, 1949. Garson Meyer and Sarah Meyer, Lester Nusbaum, Rabbis Philip Bernstein, Leon Stitskin and Stuart Rosenberg were just a few of the hundreds present. While the building was eventually torn down in 1994 to make room for the new No. 8 school, the archives of the Home contain letters and memorabilia buried in the cornerstone, none of which can be read until the year 2049. These memorabilia include messages from then Rochester mayor Samuel Dicker, Frank Gannett (founder of Gannett Newspapers), Dr. Blake McKelvey (city historian) and Clarence Gifford (president of the Rochester Community Chest), as well as many prominent people in the Jewish community. A copy of the Home's

Mort Nusbaum, a television pioneer in Rochester and president of the Home from 1965 to 67, as seen in the WHAM studio in 1948. The city and the Home were getting modern in more ways than one. Residents were some of the first folks in town to enjoy a television, donated by a generous supporter.

According to a December 1948 Old Folks *article, the residents enjoyed watching wrestling most of all. "The residents can be found grouped in their largest number on the evenings the grunt and groan boys do their stuff....Bob Turner of the WHAM-TV staff took a moment out to send greetings to the wrestling fans at the Home."*

"Dedicating the cornerstone for the new Jewish Home building became a community event. Although this building was torn down in 1994, the Home's archives still contain letters from the cornerstone that are not to be opened until the year 2049. The cornerstone itself will contain a small treasury of Rochester memorabilia—the story of the present to the future.

Included within the stone will be copies of the community's newspapers, a message from Mayor Dicker to Rochester's mayor sometime in the 21st century, messages from the president of the Home, from Frank E. Gannett, publisher of the Gannett Newspapers, from Dr. Blake McKelvey, city historian, from Arthur M. Lowenthal, president of the Jewish Community Council, from Mrs. Maurice Davidson, president of the Ladies Auxiliary of the Home, from Joseph Goldstein, president of the Council of Social Agencies, from Clarence Gifford, president of the Rochester Community Chest, and from Jesse Hannan, County Director of Social Welfare... all to their 21st Century counterparts.

Included also will be a copy of the Home constitution and by-laws, copies of Old Folks, and silver and copper coins of the day."

Old Folks, December 1949

Plans for the Home's new building appeared in the September 1948 Old Folks.

constitution and silver and copper coins of the day were also included.

As residents walked or were wheeled into their new rooms, they entered a Home that had become a model for the country—still one of the few places where need, not influence, would open doors. It was a modern, five-story brick and shell structure that included rehabilitation facilities for physical and occupational therapy, medical and dental offices, an x-ray clinic, synagogue, library, beauty shop, gift shop, dining room and lounges. It was one of the most modern and inviting homes for the aged in the nation.

I Remember

Dr. Morris Shapiro, a surgeon and longtime supporter of the Home, began volunteering there after a stint in Africa and Italy during WW II. He remembers that he and other doctors "would meet regularly to present scientific papers and socialize. These kinds of events would help us get to know one another and work together better." Dr. Shapiro recalls that these volunteers "provided a high grade of care and did the work willingly. It is Jewish tradition to care for the elderly, a basic part of the community."

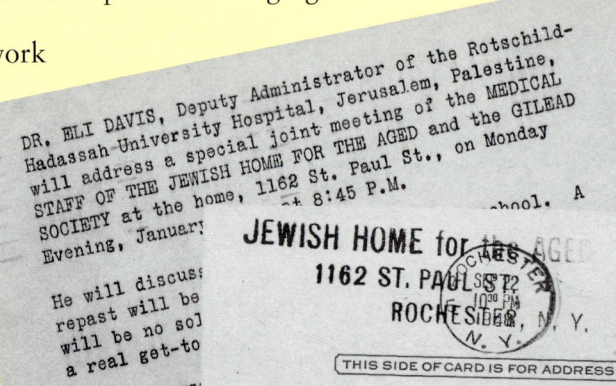

DR. ELI DAVIS, Deputy Administrator of the Rotschild-Hadassah-University Hospital, Jerusalem, Palestine, will address a special joint meeting of the MEDICAL STAFF OF THE JEWISH HOME FOR THE AGED and the GILEAD SOCIETY at the home, 1162 St. Paul St., on Monday Evening, January __ at 8:45 P.M. __hool. A

He will discuss repast will be will be no so a real get-to

WM. LIEBERTS

PLEASE

JEWISH HOME for the AGED
1162 ST. PAUL St.
ROCHESTER, N. Y.

THIS SIDE OF CARD IS FOR ADDRESS

Mr. Eli H. Rudin
1162 St. Paul Street
Rochester, N.Y.

Ladies Auxiliary

I Remember

Florence Rubens, president of the Ladies Auxiliary from 1943 to 1949, and community activist, remembers Auxiliary work in the 1940s.

"When I took over as third president, the Home was very small. We started many new projects and had a very dedicated group of members. We had a sewing group under the leadership of Tessie Shur. They made draw shirts, aprons for sale and repaired articles for the residents. The folks received Hanukkah and birthday gifts from the Auxiliary. We also provided the residents with birthday parties. We supplied them with Yiddish and English newspapers. . . . During my time, the Auxiliary was growing, so our meetings were moved from the old JYMWA building at Franklin Square to the Seneca Hotel. All these activities needed volunteers and we had a wonderful group, full of energy and devotion. We tried to make the lives of the folks more pleasant and comfortable. I think we were successful."

The Jewish Home mourned the loss of one of its earliest and most loyal supporters when Hattie Neisner died in 1949. With her husband, Joseph, Mrs. Neisner contributed in many ways, including serving on the Board and helping organize the Ladies Auxiliary. Her family's business, Neisner Brothers, made regular contributions, including hard candy and ice cream for residents. The Board praised her "intuitive feeling for the less fortunate."

The Ladies Auxiliary managed many events for the Home, including the Silver

Anniversary Dinner at the Seneca Hotel, shown here.

Courtesy Rochester Public Library

1948 continued
Synagogues are being built throughout the United States.

Brandeis University opens in Waltham, Mass.

Thanks to the JYM and WA's film service, the residents enjoy a showing of the Sholom Aleichem film, *Laughter Through Tears.*

Dr. Jose Bergara, a United Nations Fellow and chief of the Welfareville Institutions of Manila's Social Welfare Commission, inspects the Rochester Jewish Home as a guest of Home president Garson Meyer.

The Home purchases property on 26 Avenue A as living quarters for employees. The Home considers taking over Jewish Children's Home facilities on Gorham Street but decides to focus attention on a new building.

The Home hires architects Ade & Todd.

The Board signs a $250,000 mortgage at 4.5% interest from the Erie County Savings Bank of Buffalo.

The State of Israel is established.

1949
Eastman House, once the home of George Eastman, opens as public museum.

WHAM-TV makes its first television broadcast in Rochester.

Elizabeth H. L. Chase is appointed as new head nurse.

The Home creates the Board of Governors.

The Home borrows $125,000 at 3% interest from Central Trust Company in Rochester. Pledges from the 1948 campaign secure the loan.

Garson Meyer and Harold S. Rand cooperate to create a lounge for the elderly staffed by volunteers from the Federation of Church Women.

Eli H. Rudin was "accorded a signal honor at the annual conference of the New York State Social Workers. . . .when he was elected to the post of vice-president of the organization." *Old Folks*, December 1949

Central Trust Company of Rochester makes a $125,000 loan to the Home for construction costs.

Israel concludes a bilateral armistice agreement with Jordan, which terminates the military phase of the War of Independence.

"*Since there is no use fighting against nature, one might as well grow old gracefully.*"

Lin Yutang, 1939

chapter three

The Greenberg Era

"The aged must be
respected even if
only the fragments
of a once great
talent remained."

Talmud

1950 - 1984

Mrs. Vivian Cohen, Ladies Auxiliary volunteer, assisting resident Mrs. Feingold.

"When you walk into a room and someone smiles with recognition in their eyes, that is enough."

Virginia Nusbaum, Ladies Auxiliary president

Sunbathers in the garden.

In 1950, 49 men and 67 women moved into their spacious new rooms and, for the first time in many years, the Home had vacancies! It could now accommodate 153 residents and welcomed new applicants. Virginia Nusbaum, a future president (1957-59) of the Ladies Auxiliary and wife of Board president Morton Nusbaum—the son of Lester Nusbaum— remembers how the fear and anticipation in the eyes of the residents as they came in for the first time changed rapidly to looks of joy and wonder. It was a beautiful, impressive edifice!

This aerial shot of the Home is from 1952.

As the Home grew in size, it became more professional in its operations. Board committees began doing self-appraisals and recommended improvements. Admissions policies were revised, requiring that women had to be 60 or older, men 65 and older. For the first time, the Home also agreed to accept non-Jewish spouses of Jewish applicants—a sign that it was accommodating to the changing realities of the Jewish community even though its dietary laws would continue to be strictly kosher and Friday evenings and Saturday Sabbath would continue to be respected, as they are to this day.

Eli Rudin in his office in 1950.

Residents enjoying sitting in the Falk Lounge of the St. Paul Street Home.

Women to the Rescue

The Ladies Auxiliary consisted of over 1,000 dues-paying members in the early 1950s. There were also 100 volunteers, who did everything from visiting residents to baking cakes on special

Auxiliary Sabbath tea in the Neisner Room, presided over by Virginia Nusbaum, Rose Wolfe, Helen Grossman, Hilda Wolk and Rhoda Rappaport.

occasions. Essie Cohen Germanow began her involvement volunteering in the physical therapy department. She became president in 1953 and has remained active ever since. Since 1985, she has chaired a committee responsible for purchasing and collecting art for the new facility on South Winton Road. Pinny Cooke made her mark in the 1950s, before starting her political career in the New York State Assembly, "making life a little better" for the residents. She recalls

wonderful times at fashion shows, song fests and luncheons. She also remembers working with outstanding women like Rose Wolfe (president, 1960-62) and Beatrice Goran (president, 1964-66), who devoted so much of their lives to the Home. "One can't think of the Sabbath teas without recalling the ever-present Rose," she notes. Then there was the "Monday Morning Group," composed of Ann Natapow, Edith Goldstein and Bea Metzger, who would work with the most difficult patients on the infirmary floor to supplement the nursing care. Later in the decade, others took their turn—women like Ethel Kowal (president, 1967-68), who also became president of the Home (1988-90), Sylvia Berman, Nathalie Goldberg (president 1962-64) and wife of future Board president Emanuel Goldberg (1971-73), and Min Edelman (president, 1969-70). As one volunteer

remarked, this kind of work, which enhanced the lives of the residents and added to their dignity and joy, certainly was characterized "by some *tzores* [trouble] but an awful lot of *naches* [gratification]."

Judge Jacob Ark flanked by Virginia Nusbaum and Rose Wolfe.

As it grew in size and scope, the Auxiliary also became increasingly professional in its operations, conducting itself like an independent non-profit organization. It held general membership meetings

Auxiliary function.

*Auxiliary
Luncheon
served by Virginia
Nusbaum,
Rose Wolfe
and Ceil Loeb.*

quarterly, elected its own Board of Directors, and funded special projects ranging from purchasing a station wagon to transport residents to outings and visits to physicians, to funding a beauty shop where seniors could get their hair and nails done, to birthday celebrations and Mother's and Father's Day gifts, to acquiring special new equipment. Volunteers took charge of hosting Saturday teas, a ritual during which they served coffee, tea, sodas and homemade cookies and cakes to residents and their friends and family. The Auxiliary also set up a shopping service for residents.

The reward for their work was, as Shirley Axelrod (president, 1971-74) remarked, "to see little bits of improvement." Ginni Nusbaum agreed. "When you walk into a room and someone smiles with recognition in their eyes, that is enough." Ethel Kowal was speaking for all volunteers when she recounted the

About WOMEN

April 10, 52

Grandmother at 92 Young in Spirit

By Pat Barry

AT 92, Sarah Meyer is older than most of the old.

Perhaps that is why a visit from this independent little woman is inspiration for the aging to whom living is sometimes a lonely, wearying chore.

Last Sunday, I joined Mrs. Meyer and her son, Garson, on a tour of the Jewish Home for the Aged, an institution she helped found in 1921 and of which her son is now president.

Mrs. Meyer is a small lady—barely 5 feet tall. She wore a long white shawl around her neck, and kept her hands clasped together most

of the time. I rarely heard her speak, except for a few Hebrew words of greeting to this one and that one of the oldsters who clamored for her attention.

"Please," begged an eager old person, "please, come for Seder with us."

"I must, Mrs. Meyer, have two hours to talk with you," announced a spectacled woman.

"Would you come to my room next—to see the things I've made?" asked another.

Here and there, an oldster drew her aside for a few minutes of gossip —usually one-sided, since Mrs. Meyer is a gifted listener. In the infirmary ward, she spoke even less, but her touch seemed to give comfort to the blind, voiceless, paralyzed and to those whose memories are fading. She shook hands endlessly in sunrooms, corridors, and even in the kitchen.

It was a trek her son and I never finished. After an hour we tired, and went to find comfortable chairs in the lounge, while the sprightly "little grandmother," as most folks call her, went on, cheering those who wanted cheer, attending to the ones who needed sympathetic companionship.

The little grandmother, I learned from her son, is impelled by an astonishing vitality and spiritual warmth to live life at a clip that would enfeeble persons half her age. The Home for the Aged, rejuvinated a year ago with a fabulously modern building, is one of her favorite beats because she is responsible for its existence.

Besides, she belongs to nearly a dozen Jewish women's groups devoted to old-fashioned charity as well as modern social relief. Nearly every evening, Meyer said, she stops by Agudas Achim Nusach Ary— the Morris St. synagogue—"in case there's a meeting." The telephone in her plain little cottage on Joseph Ave. is the terminal of an efficient grapevine system sensitive to the needs of her community.

A baby is to be born: Mrs. Meyer is at hand with whatever is needed. A family falls into hard times: she makes a brief appearance at the public market and presently a basket of food is delivered to the hungry. An old soul is lonely: the little grandmother soon sits by the bedside, listening, nodding and smiling. Death comes to an old Jewish woman: she goes at once to perform the ritual that few are qualified to do any more.

"I'm lucky if I find her home," remarked her son. He admits that the attempts of her family (6 sons and daughters, 16 grandchildren and 20 great-grandchildren) to supervise her activities are ineffectual. "I telephoned one night at midnight to tell her I was going out of town unexpectedly. She wasn't home—out tending to somebody or other, I suppose."

Tonight, Jews will sit down to Seder, the ceremonial meal of Passover, most joyous of all Jewish holidays. Special foods and goodies require days to prepare. Any stranger who knocks at the door during the celebration is welcomed and fed.

"My mother has hinted already that she will be needing some extension tables and a lot of folding chairs," Meyer told me Sunday. "She will have about 15 people for Seder. She never waits for the strangers to knock on the door. She hunts them up ahead of time."

emotions she felt after her hand was warmly grasped and kissed by a resident. "I have no words to tell you of my feelings. It is such a pleasure to work with our residents—accept their blessing and feel you should do more to be worthy."

As the Auxiliary became increasingly vital to the soul and operations of the Home, its president regularly attended the Home's board meetings.

Volunteerism Grows

Auxiliary women were not the only ones who donated hours of time and energy to the Home. Hundreds of men and women from the Rochester community contributed their time and expertise, doing everything from raising money to giving informal talks to residents. One of the most dedicated of these volunteers was Samuel Ball, a former treasurer of the Board. He owned a shoe repair shop on Clinton Avenue but made it his business to visit the residents every Tuesday. At a testimonial dinner given in his honor, Garson Meyer remarked, "Most of us can make a living

Auxiliary Sabbath tea. The volunteers include Phyllis Davidson, Helen Nusbaum, Rose Wolfe and Gladys Buff.

in less than all of our wakeful hours. How we use the remainder of our time determines the grace and value of our lives. Samuel Ball has given selflessly to the Home for most of his life."

Volunteers performed a wide variety of services and did much to enrich the lives of those in the Home. Anna Goldstein did crafts with the residents for over twenty years until she herself became a resident. Mickey Furman, Minnie Briskin, Ann Epstein, Tessie Shur, Bessie Friedman, Ida Kaplan, Betty Grossman, Evalyn Phillips, Vivian Cohen, Ruth and Lou Osband, and Annette and Sy Osband were devoted volunteers who provided the day-to-day, "hands-on" work with the residents that made life better for them. Led by Max Kravetz, individuals including Manny Hoffman and Al Rudman helped out with the *shul* (the Eber Synagogue was part of the new structure, and Allen Eber provided the ritual

I Remember

Essie Germanow, dedicated volunteer and former Auxiliary president (1953-55), remembers her early association with the Home.

"I initially got involved with the Home because my mother and many of her friends were among the early volunteers at the Home. My mother's uncle—my great uncle—was a resident there many years ago at the original old home on St. Paul Street. I would go with her to visit him. It was always pointed out that we had a responsibility to the elderly and that to support this institution in our community was essential.

"I served as a volunteer for many years in the physical therapy department—as well as occupational therapy—and often drove the residents to their summer picnics at the Idlers Club and elsewhere. I will never forget the greeting I always received from one of the dear little ladies in the occupational therapy room. There she was, her fingers so gnarled and crippled with arthritis—yet with the sweetest smile—she'd greet me with 'Hello, beauty!' That was one of the many bonuses I received as a volunteer!"

I Remember

Pinny Cooke captures the following memories of her involvement with the Auxiliary.

"We moved to Rochester in 1952. Margie Cooke Taylor, our first child, was two years old. Essie Germanow was an old friend who took me to Don & Bob's at the lake for a hamburger with 'everything' and talked about her work at the Jewish Home. I joined the Ladies Auxiliary, as it was then known, became a member of the Board and followed Essie as president in 1957.

"In 1956 my grandmother, who had raised me, suffered a stroke. Eli Rudin, the executive director at the Home, permitted me to bring her to the Home from Syracuse. I was pregnant with our third child and I was later able to bring the baby to the home to visit. At that time Rose Wolfe was also on the Board. She would call me early in the morning to discuss the menu for our luncheons. I can still hear her voice—'Tuna fish, egg salad or what?'

"Bea Goran was also on the Board, and we formed the 1180 Club around that time. Our fashion shows were second to none. We all wore our own clothes! We had dances and shows and so much fun, and we bought a station wagon for the Home. I think it was blue. I know it was the first.

"We were the first non-smoking area also. Rae Edelstein couldn't stand the smoke and those of us who smoked [then] went out into the hall. We were so advanced!

"I loved all of those moments—I cherish those memories."

residents or were available for a good *schmooz* (conversation).

When David Lazeroff, an active board member and former treasurer, died several years later, the Home dedicated two stained glass windows in the synagogue in his honor, establishing a precedent to honor men and women who rendered a lifetime of outstanding service to the Home.

Dr. Eli A. Leven (left) presenting Joe E. Silverstein with a

Board resolution acknowledging years of devoted service.

wine as well as visiting every Sunday and donating fresh fruits for the picnics); Moe Trott came for services every *Yom Tov* and was responsible for the *yahrzeit* plaques; Abe Cohen and his wife, Ethel, would play Yiddish records on the stereo system donated by Myron "Mike" Silver; Louis Rappaport and Norman King arranged to secure a projector for the Home; Jay Golden (manager of the Palace Theater and Board member),

provided first-run films that were shown by Jack Parsky and Philip Kaplan; and countless others would read to the

An annual residents picnic.

The dedication of the Eber synagogue.

Crushed Grapes

But Board members and volunteers were not the only ones singled out for their outstanding contributions to Jewish life. Henrietta Posner, a resident, published a book of poetry in 1954, *Crushed Grapes*, that she had composed while a resident of the Home. Her care at the Home had been a great incentive to completing this work. Her sons, Mitchel and Joe U. Posner, have been long-standing supporters of the Home.

New Infirmary

A number of men and women in the Home were intellectually active and able to read, write and carry on meaningful conversations. But an increasing percentage were partly bedridden and seriously ill. By the mid-1950s, almost half of all residents needed infirmary care—a ratio that would continue for several years—making it necessary to expand the medical facilities. "The crowded conditions in the Infirmary have taken away the flexibility of the bed arrangement, making it difficult to secure emergency rooms when contagious or terminal cases make it necessary," reported Dr. Eli Leven (the Home's first employed medical director), to the Board in 1952. "There is a great turnover of staff, but usually 25 employees care for about 70 patients, in addition to providing care for the ambulant floors. This is completely out of proportion with general hospitals, which are basically providing the same care with considerably more help."

In response, the Board, under the leadership of president Ruben Dankoff, decided to expand and once again went to the Erie Savings Bank in Buffalo, seeking a loan of $280,000. The money would be used to add an additional 60-bed infirmary wing.

The Home also became involved in medical research projects involving the treatment of the elderly. One of the first was a study on Thorazine, a major new tranquilizer, undertaken by Smith, Kline & French. Through the intervention of Dr. Benjamin Pollack, a Board member and assistant administrator of the Rochester State Hospital, a number of patients who had been in that hospital for ten to twenty years suffering from severe mental disorders were able to be transferred to the Home, a benefit not only to researchers but to these individuals, who found a familial atmosphere for the first time in many years.

"One of the men who came to us from this project had been a back ward patient at the Rochester State Hospital for many many

years," recalled Will Greenberg, then assistant director, in an article in the *Jewish Ledger*. "He was a short, bearded gentleman; very shy and quiet. As a matter of fact, I can't remember hearing him speak! But, I did see him sitting in the synagogue reading over his books the better part of every day. It makes you feel good inside to experience this." There is also the case of a "Mrs. R," who was now able to make aprons and earn money. She brought some of that money to Greenberg to pay for her *yahrzeit* and bronze plaque. "I don't want I should bother the children," she said in her

heavy Yiddish accent.

In 1954, the construction of the addition to the infirmary was completed, raising the capacity of the Home to 215 and prompting the Home to change its name to The Jewish Home and Infirmary of Rochester, Inc.

The Jewish Home Board in 1952. Standing in left rear, moving right and then seated left to right, are Harold Rand, David Lazeroff, Ben Robfogel, Jacob Ark, Max Cohen, Ruben Dankoff, Samuel Greenhouse, Helen Nusbaum, Ben Leve, J. Heller, Sol Levin, Garson Meyer, Eli Rudin, Joe Silverstein, Herman Cohn, Joseph Goldstein, Ben Pollack, Robert Markus, and Harry Germanow.

Tests at Jewish Home
New Drug Benefits Aged

2/18/55

By JACK VAN BUREN

Thorazine, a new drug that has shown great promise in the relief of mental disorders at Rochester State Hospital, is now being used to improve the well-being of elderly persons at the Jewish Home for the Aged.

Within the last three weeks, the drug has been administered to 27 selected residents of the home, who have been restless, excited, somewhat confused, and who did not eat or sleep properly. No one in the group is a mental patient, although most suffer from physical ailments associated with old age.

Twenty of the 27 have shown marked improvement since taking the drug. They eat and sleep better, are calmer, more agreeable and sociable, and in general, take a renewed interest in life.

Results Not Conclusive

Doctors emphasized, however, that because of the short period of time covered by the experiment, the results cannot be interpreted as conclusive. It may be several months or a year before final conclusions can be drawn.

But if the initial results hold up, the drug may become an important new tool in caring for an ever increasing population of older persons. Rochester, for example, which is dotted with organized homes for the elderly, has one of the highest proportion of persons above 65 in the nation.

The experiment at the Jewish Home, located at 1180 St. Paul St., was launched at the suggestion of Dr. Benjamin Pollack, assistant director of Rochester State Hospital. He is a member of the Home's board of directors. Dr. Pollack has been directing the experiment at the state hospital.

Supervising of Tests

At the Home, the test is being supervised by Dr. Eli A. Leven, medical staff; Dr. Gustav Rosenthal, physician; Mrs. Elizabeth Lane, director of nurses; and Eli Rudin, executive director.

NEW TEST—Those pellets held by Nurse Elaine Knopf are thorazine pills, whose use on elderly folks at Jewish Home for the Aged already shows good results in their physical well-being after only a three-week trial.

thorazine, he didn't sleep much, had a poor appetite, was excitable and constantly complained. Now, said Mrs. Chase, he is "like a new man." He eats and sleeps well, doesn't complain and is generally given, in the beginning, and gradually this is cut down to minimum dose.

Referring to the results as "satisfactory," Dr. Pollack, who is cooperating in the study, said results so far have been "truly good." Here are two typical cases:

One was taking the drug, a patient, grouchy, unhappy, restless, and apparently unhappy. Since taking the drug, Mrs. Chase said, he is happy, calmer and the drug made the difference.

According to...

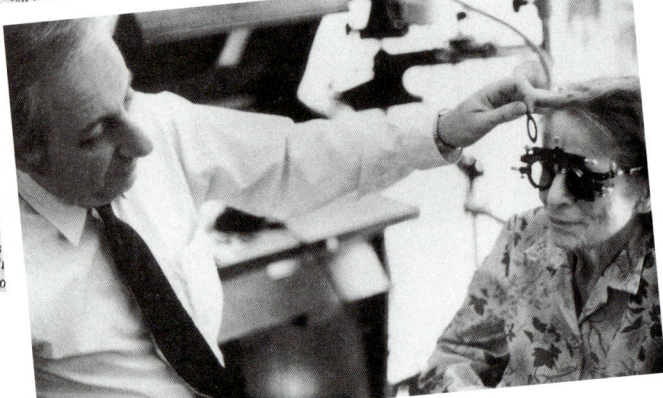

The Greenberg Era

Will Greenberg, trained as a social worker, took over as director in 1957, when Eli Rudin assumed the executive position of the Hebrew Home for the Aged of Boston. Greenberg held that position until 1984. He inherited an institution that was progressive, patient oriented, and in a physical structure that was ahead of most homes for the aged at that time. He also brought a certain sensibility of caring, Jewish warmth and compassion, probably nurtured in the Rochester Jewish Children's Home, where he was a resident from 1926 to 1936. His goal, like those before him, was to see

Ophthalmologist Dr. Joe Silverberg performing a test on a resident.

Man Is Not Alone, by Abraham Joshua Heschel, is published.

1952
Life expectancy in the United States is 67 years for men and more than 71 years for women.

Movement of the U.S. Jewish population to the suburbs gains momentum.

1953
The Home's new building houses 153 people.

1954
An additional 50 beds open at the Home, bringing the total number of residents to 240.

American Jews celebrate the tercentenary of Jewish settlement in the United States.

William Greenberg becomes assistant director of the Home.

The Home participates in a research project sponsored by Smith, Kline & French, for the use of Thorazine. According to William Greenberg, "This enabled us to accept Jewish men and women who had been patients at the Rochester State Hospital for 10 and 20 years. How gratifying was the success of this project to the patients, families, and our staff, who helped these persons 'come our of their shells' and blossom as individuals." *Jewish Ledger*, December 6, 1954

Approximately 2,000 non-Jews are being converted to Judaism annually.

1955
The Home's name changes to "Jewish Home and Infirmary of Rochester, Inc."

"what we could do to make life as meaningful for the residents as possible" and to see "how far we could bring people." It was an exciting time with many accomplishments.

The new infirmary wing, which opened in 1954, allowed the Home to provide more services for the chronically ill and disabled and to receive more funding from the Community Chest, now the United Way. The growth of medical services and personnel also made it possible for the Home to revise its mission from a near-hospice institution to a facility that genuinely extended lives by providing rehabilitative services and varied social and cultural programming. Some of the residents benefiting from short-term care were relatively young, in their mid-forties. Others were elderly and needed a comforting place to recover after critical operations, accidents, strokes and other acute but remediable conditions. By 1960, over a quarter of the residents in the Home were able to return to their families for home care, and many of these people were in their 70s and 80s.

As the demand for services increased, new emphasis, under the guidance of Dr. Leven, was placed on developing state-of-the-art occupational and physical therapy programs, now significant features of the services provided by the Home. Pauline Spitulnik (later Pauline Kaplan) was engaged as a trained physical therapist and did a great deal to professionalize this department. Later, Judy Lurie came on staff and continued this high level of care for over thirty years. She is still very involved with the Home as a volunteer.

The Home also refined its hospitalization services, developing its own medical lab for routine blood and urine tests, increasing the number of registered nurses on its staff so

The Old Folks

New Addition To Home Completed

Vol. VII, No. 2   A Publication of the Jewish Home For The Aged, Rochester, N. Y.   October, 1954

New Wing Increases Home to 215 Bed Total

More Funds Needed To Pay

The new 64 bed addition to the Home is now complete. With the beginning of the New Year, members of the Home for the Aged can be thankful that Rochester Jewry now have the additional modern facilities to care for their aging and infirm parents ... ood the care and treatment the Jewish Home affords.

... buildings on the present site offered crowded quar- ... ficially dedicated. The

Arthur Cerasoni, the art instructor, with enthusiastic resident students.

A 1957 meeting of the Board of Directors. Included are Robert Markin, Dr. Ben Pollack, Judge Jacob Ark, Harry Cornell, Florence Rubens, Maurice Forman, Sol Levin, Joseph Silverstein, Max Lapides, Leon Sturman, Sam Poze, Sam Ball, Essie Germanow, Dr. Eli Leven, Virginia Nusbaum, Mort Nusbaum, Harold Rand, Lou Glassman, and Joseph Goldstein. Samuel Greenhouse and Will Greenberg are in front.

there would be one per floor, and setting up a dental and podiatry clinic. Dr. Michael Kowal was very influential in developing dental care for the residents. He was assisted by the generous support of Dr. Garson Rosenthal, Dr. Paul Garfinkel and the members of the Alpha Omega dental fraternity. Soon, the Home was accepted as a member of the American Hospital Association.

Under Board president Samuel H. Greenhouse's leadership (1956-58), the social and cultural programs of the Home were also enriched. Greenhouse arranged with the Rochester Board of Education to provide an adult education program for residents. Arthur Cerasoni held art classes every week and residents drew pastels and made watercolor pictures, many of which were put on display. Frances Fox, the legendary English teacher at Monroe High School, taught English and history classes a few times a week in the library. These classes were very significant and gratifying for the participants, since so many were foreign born and had limited formal education. One grandmother was beaming with pride when she

1180 Club Is Born

Oldsters Frolic at Open House

Residents of the Jewish Home and Infirmary were "at home" yesterday to friends from all over the city at the first meeting of the 1180 Club.

They entertained their guests in one of the center's spacious lounges where bridge tables had been set up for games and refreshments. As the afternoon progressed, one of the "hostesses" seated herself at a baby grand piano in the corner and picked out a snatch of ragtime.

In a few minutes, the entire assembly was singing the old favorites, led by the chairman of the entertainment program, Mrs. Charles Goran.

The idea for the club started out quite casually with the suggestion of one of the home's residents to entertain elderly citizens from the neighborhood at an afternoon of games and conversation. Name for the group was inspired by the address of the home—1180 St. Paul St.

As plans for the open house expanded, it was decided to extend a general invitation to the community, with the thought of organizing a senior citizen's club which would meet weekly. Administrators agreed that social contacts among the guests at the home and elderly citizens in the neighborhood would broaden the interests of all concerned.

A total attendance of some 80 persons at the first get-together encouraged the planners to look toward future programs which will consist of films, music, card games and varied entertainment.

HIGH NOTES—Entertaining guests with music at the Jewish Home and Infirmary are, from the left: Mrs. Rose Weinstein, at piano; Mrs. Charles Goran, chairman of the 1180 Club, named for address of the home at 1180 St. Paul St.; and Jacob Buff. Club entertains area residents.

completed a letter in English to her grandson in college. Another resident learned to spell his name. There was a graduation celebration every year on the patio. In 1963, for example, Adult Education Certificates of Merit were given to 67 residents ranging in age from 65 to 90. When the Board of Education could no longer subsidize the program, the Home Board agreed to support the project until other funds were available.

It was also during this period, in 1955, that the Ladies Auxiliary established the "1180 Club" as a coffee shop serving refreshments once a week to residents and their families. Plans were made to establish the canteen that ultimately became the Café Shalom. Life at the Home went on.

Life at the Home

The Home was an active place and the residents, on the whole, engaged with each other and staff to form a viable social community. The sense of one's mortality by some mysterious process, and the encouragement and love of staff, friends and relatives, made every moment matter. Life at the Home was passionate, energetic, and

1955 continued
The Conference of Presidents of Major American Jewish Organizations is organized.

1957
William Greenberg becomes the director of the Home.

1961
The old Jewish Home building at 1162 St. Paul is razed.

Janet Feenstra, instructor in the occupational therapy room, reorganizes the gift shop.

Night, the English version of *Un di velt hot geshvign* by Elie Wiesel, is published.

Adolf Eichmann is put on trial in Jerusalem for crimes against the Jewish people and humanity.

The Second Vatican Council convened by Pope John XXIII begins.

At the annual Hanukkah sale, all items are made by residents of the Home and include pocketbooks, aprons, dolls, ash trays, jewelry, and many other "practical and lovely gifts." Half of the purchase price of every item is returned to the resident who made the gift. *Auxiliary Newsletter*, October 1961

1964
Three civil rights workers, Michael Schwerner, Andrew Goodman, and James Cheney, are murdered in Mississippi.

*Residents cele-
brating in the
sukkah,* led by
Cantor Hersh
Friedman.

*Dr. Eli Leven
thanking members
of the Rochester
Jewish Relief*

*Organization for
their ongoing
support to the
Home.*

infused with *Yiddish tam.* For instance, there was always something special in the air on Fridays and on the eve of Jewish holidays. The sweet aromas of the *Shabbat* meal, prepared expertly by chef David vonPerlstein (1963-1976), permeated the Home, adding to the special atmosphere. The Sabbath is the most sacred of Jewish holy days. On the Sabbath, tradition teaches, a Jew enters paradise on earth. The woman, in lighting the candles, brings the foretaste of paradise into her environment. On *Shabbat*, some say, the Jew has an extra soul. One still senses that spirit in the Home.

Residents are not always easy people to help. Feelings of pride and the need for autonomy are strong, despite their physical frailties and illnesses. They still see themselves as givers, not takers, and the Home staff and volunteers devote enormous energies to fostering a sense of independence, action, and decision making. The Residents' Council provides a venue for expression and action. Continuous diverse programs are offered— cultural events, discussions, classes, bingo, music—along with social affairs, religious ceremonies, celebrations,

I Remember

Irving Kessler, member of the Board from 1955 to 1970 and one of the founders of the Jewish Home Foundation, reflects on his involvement with the Home.

"I was bar mitzvahed at the Home. I am the youngest of four brothers and three of us were bar mitzvahed there in the late 1920s and early 1930s. This took place in the original building of the Home. The synagogue was downstairs and in the back. Given the fact that it was the Depression, my bar mitzvah was not very lavish. There was *kichel* and herring and some sponge cake. I have fond memories of these early days, people sitting on the porch, rocking and reading, the *benching* of the Friday night *licht,* the men sitting around a long table in the synagogue, engaged in animated discussion concerning some Jewish text. It was a very friendly, inviting place—a home.

"That spirit was still evident when I got involved on the Board level. Samuel H. Greenhouse was the first president I served under. He owned a ladies dress shop on Main Street near the Four Corners. I was on the committee that reviewed all the applications of people who wanted to enter the Home. We would meet in an office in the back of his shop. Usually children came on behalf of their parent. While we tried to make the best arrangement possible for the Home, no one was ever turned away. These meetings were often difficult, but everyone received proper consideration. We knew what was at stake."

anniversaries, birthdays, memorials, and an occasional wedding. The gamut of political and social processes found outside the Home is present there as well. Here is an entire, though miniature, society, the setting for a rich Jewish culture, made up of bits and pieces of people's common history and shared *Yiddishkeyt.*

Will Greenberg devoted himself to "his people" for over thirty years. Sometimes he was a surrogate son, sometimes a worrying, protective parent to them. A social worker by training, with a huge heart, he watched over the elders' health, listened to their complaints, mediated their quarrels, made sure the soup was not too hot or too

LONG WAY FROM HOME?—Humane Society representatives yesterday identified this homing pigeon, found in the court of the Jewish Home for the Aged by 89-year-old Max Rosenthal, left, as property of a Honolulu fancier. Local breeder Patrick Marzulo, 46 Woodward St., right, will nurse the exhausted bird until its broken leg heals. Marzulo doubts if the bird flew such a distance, but says it's a good pigeon.

At Home

cold, too thick or thin, encouraged them when they lost heart and provided for them, insisting that they continue to survive, that life is worth living. He represented the spirit, the *neshama*, of the Home—the skills and technologies of the new informed by the enduring values of the past.

Longevity: A Mixed Blessing

When the Home opened in 1920, the average life span of a man was 56 and a woman was 59. By 1960, the average life span extended to 68 for men and 74 for women. By 1993, it reached 73 for men and 79 for women. Clearly, longevity was a boon to scores of these elderly men and women, who were able to enjoy what seemed to be endless *mitzvahs*: births of grandchildren and great grandchildren, weddings, bar and bat mitzvahs, graduations

Annual meeting of the Board in the early 1960s. From left to right are Charles Kell- manson, Herbert Mock, Allen Eber, Paul Brennen, and Irving Kessler.

The 1961 demolition of the original Home. Standing left to right are Herman Schwartz, Mort Nusbaum, Allen Eber, Justice Jacob Ark, Garson Meyer, Samuel Green- house, and Emanuel Goldberg.

1965
The Auxiliary presents a theater party at the Dryden Theatre.

Sandy Koufax, Los Angeles Dodger, sets a record with his fourth no-hit game in four years.

Medicaid and Medicare take effect.

1967
The Six Day War shakes the Jewish community. Jerusalem is united, and the Western Wall liberated.

1968
The State Mental Health Department changes the course of events for all nursing homes. One could no longer admit patients

to the state hospital simply because they were old, difficult to manage at home, or there was no place for them in the community.

The Reconstructionist Rabbinical College is opened in Philadelphia.

1969
An addition to the Home makes 60 more beds available.

The Conservative movement establishes the first Havurah group in Somerville, Mass.

1971
Eli Rudin helps create the Regional Council on Aging.

1970s
The media exposes Rabbi Berman for abuse in his New York City nursing home. Investigations begin in homes throughout the state.

Aaron Braveman leads discussion groups at the Jewish Home and St. John's Home.

1973
The Yom Kippur War awakens the consciousness of American Jews and reaffirms the importance of Jewish commitment.

1973 continued
The Rabbinical Assembly, the organization of Conservative rabbis, rule that women may be counted for a *minyan*.

1974
New Horizons Day Care Program, a daytime social program for seniors, begins at the Jewish Home, the first of its kind in Monroe County. According to a brochure for the program, "Life-long learning and independent decision making

are primary goals of the program. New Horizons activities are designed around the arts and humanities, discussions of world events, and community outings."

Oscar Schindler, a German industrialist who saved more than 1,500 Jews during the Holocaust, dies.

1978
The Home's budget is over $3.5 million. Food costs $600,000. Drugs cost $600,000. Capacity: Skilled Nursing Facility (SNF) 176 beds. Health Related Facility 66 beds. The charge for SNF is $53 a day. The charge for HRF is $31.50 a day.

Isaac Bashevis Singer is awarded the Nobel Prize for Literature.

March 2 is Italian Night in the Home's dining room.

The Camp David Agreement between Israel and Egypt is signed.

1979
The Home drops plans for a senior citizens' apartment complex plan in Brighton, citing community opposition and property restrictions as the reasons.

William Greenberg celebrates 25 years with the Jewish Home.

and all sorts of family get-togethers.

But for others, those added years brought additional illnesses and infirmities. Many managed to survive heart attacks, strokes and terrible infections, only to become victims of terrifying afflictions that had no cure, ranging from dementia and Alzheimer's to Parkinson's.

Demographic studies of the Jews of Rochester were conducted in 1960 and 1980. The surveys disclose that the population remained relatively stable at approximately 22,000, with the number of households increasing but the number per household going down. This indicates the decline of the extended family and the increase of persons living alone. The age distribution also changed significantly, the median age rising from 38 to 43. In 1960, the percent of those above 65 was 13; by 1980, it had increased to 19.1. This had a definite impact on the Home.

The official invitation to the 40th Anniversary and Annual Meeting.

Under the leadership of presidents Justice Jacob Ark (1958-61), Dr. Eli Leven (1962-64), Morton Nusbaum (1965-67), Leon Germanow (1968-70), and Emanuel Goldberg (1971-73), the role of the Home in the community was changing to meet these demographic changes in the Jewish and general community.

State Supreme Court Justice Ark, the uncle of Adelaide Weinberg, noted as early as 1962 that "the Home was evolving into a facility for the care of the chronically ill rather than a residence center for the aged." It was also moving in the direction of becoming a rehabilitation center for convalescent care.

By 1967, almost one-third of the residents in the Home suffered from some type of mental illness and needed specialists who could treat them. As a result, the Home added several psychiatrists to its staff, as well as nurses trained to help disoriented residents dress, communicate and eat.

Expansion

When the State Mental Health Department decreed that patients could no longer be admitted to state hospitals simply because they were old, unable to care for themselves and bereft of family, the Home was one of the few places in the Rochester area able to treat this population. More space again became a priority, and in 1967 planning began for the construction of a new medical wing to accommodate increasing demand for medical services in anticipation of the recently passed Medicaid and Medicare programs. At that point, the Home was serving an average of 172 persons daily with a staff of 123, over half of whom were working in the infirmary providing 24-hour nursing and medical care. Once again, the Board and the Jewish community came through. Under the leadership of Morton Nusbaum, Leon Germanow, Benjamin Robfogel, Joseph Silverstein,

---

I Remember

Leon Germanow, president of the Board from 1968 to 70, reflects on his presidency.

"My predecessor was Morton Nusbaum. The meetings used to be quite lengthy. Morton, being a radio personality, someone who loved to talk and talked well, had long meetings. When I became president, the first thing I said to the board was that our meetings would start at 7:30 and end promptly at 9:30. Needless to say, I was a very popular president. I also remember fondly our working luncheon meetings. Our cook, David vonPerlstein, could cook like a dream. I would ask him to prepare a plain sandwich. David did not know what a plain sandwich was. He was a master chef.

"More seriously, it was in this period that we decided as a board to enlarge our infirmary. We needed to put on a new wing with sixty beds. The question arose, of course, where would we get the money, the two million dollars needed for this ambitious project. I can recall the meeting where this was discussed. Everybody suddenly got quiet. Since I was on the board of Monroe Savings Bank, I told the Jewish Home board that I would handle it. I approached the bank at its next board meeting. As the only Jewish member, I asked for a few minutes to make the case for a substantial loan 'tomorrow' so that we could get started. Maybe they felt they couldn't refuse their only Jewish member. The next day the loan was approved.

"I quickly put together a capital campaign committee headed by Joseph Silverstein and Emanuel Goldberg. They managed to raise about one million dollars in a very short period of time. We also received a major gift from Mr. Lawrence Wagner, who was not Jewish. God must have been on our side. At the dedication of the Germanow-Simon Activities Center, I remember saying: 'The sun has shone upon us and we want to share the sun with you.' That tradition of responsibility and thankfulness I passed on to my capable successor, Manny Goldberg."

and Emanuel Goldberg, money was borrowed and raised. Leon Germanow helped secure a substantial loan from Monroe Savings Bank, on whose board he sat, and a group of Board members came forward to secure that loan. The new wing was opened in

Vol. XIII, No. 1   A Publication of the Jewish Home and Infirmary, Rochester, N. Y.   December, 1964

MODERNIZATION OF HOME IN PROGRESS

EMPHASIS TO BE PLACED ON "THE NEW LOOK"

Sensitive to changing times, and striving continuously to provide the maximum in comfort and dignity for the residents, a large scale program of modernization has been embarked upon after many months of study.

The pounding of hammers and drills, the ringing of copper tubing, and the clatter of falling plaster echoes throughout the Home today as the vision of the Board of Directors is fulfilled in concrete action.

The basic human desire for privacy is being given the highest priority in the renovation program and alterations are taking place, which because of lack of funds, could not be provided in the original building. The number of single rooms for residents and patients is being increased two and one-half fold by conversion of double rooms into single rooms wherever structurally possible. A major plumbing project is also under way in this emphasis upon privacy, and a majority of the rooms will be equipped with private toilet facilities.

Dr. Eli A. Leven, Home President, signs renovation contracts.

As part of the over-all plan and in recognition of the changing needs of the residents, a nursing station is to be built on the third floor. The vision of the original architects of the building facilitates this alteration as the future need for such a nursing station was planned for in the first blueprints. Included in the plans is the installation of the most modern electronic call system on the infirmary floors to insure the simplest but most effective patient-nurse communication. Through this call system the patient can instantaneously make his needs known to the nurse who can then render the most efficient service.

Separate cheerful dining areas will also be provided on the Infirmary floors to overcome the monotony of patients being served all their meals in their rooms by tray.

The long felt need for a pharmacy room will also be met in the present planning. The service of a Pharmacist on the Staff will not only provide more efficient drug distribution but will also result in overall economies. The establishment of central supply areas will also result in further staff and administrative efficiencies to better serve our residents.

An enlarged Physical Therapy Department is also part of the new blueprints. With a larger area in which to operate, it will be possible to provide further specialized treatments. This will also open the way to possible establishment of an outpatient physical therapy service.

The warmth of the Home will be enhanced by the installation of the most modern electrical fixtures and complete interior decoration in colors that will blend with the new decor. Carpeting in corridors and lounges is also envisaged to enrich the new look. "It is our belief," said President Dr. Eli A. Leven, "that the Jewish Community will point with pride to their new Jewish Home as being a model for geriatric institutions."

Members of the Building Committee of the Board studying blueprints of "The New Look"

An artist's conception of a refurbished lounge designed to enhance the social life of the residents.

The renovation of the 1180 St. Paul Street building in the early 1960s.

The 1961 demolition of the original Home.

November 1969, adding 60 beds and bringing the total capacity of the Home to 242 residents. The medical wing was named the Lawrence Wagner Wing after a generous bequest from his estate. The new activities center, which allowed the Home to reach out to the non-resident population to help them stay in the community, was named the Germanow-Simon Activities Center. The trends influencing the Home to become more and more of a comprehensive medical center for the elderly continued to intensify.

Nursing Home Renaissance

By 1973, three-fourths of the residents in the Home needed infirmary care. Many were subsidized by Medicare and Medicaid. The growth of these new programs enabled the Rochester Home—and many others nationwide—to

1979 continued

The Home begins plans to relocate and sends a letter outlining these intentions to Arnold S. Gissin, then area administrator for the State Department of Health.

The Presidential Commission on the Holocaust, created in 1978 and headed by Elie Wiesel, holds its first meeting.

1980s

The Ladies Auxiliary changes its name to the Jewish Home Auxiliary and admits its first male member, Manny Hoffman.

Ruth B. Rosenberg is the Home's first female president.

1981

The Three Day Health Care Program begins at the Home.

The Home exercises an option to purchase 20 acres of land fronting on South Winton Road in the Town of Brighton.

Irving Lamm, former executive director of the Jewish Home for the Aged of Rhode Island, in Providence, is named administrator, replacing William J. Greenberg, who takes the position of director of special projects.

1982

Professor Kelly Beller, who teaches "Options for Jewish Learning" classes at the Home, says, "In many of the nursing homes, they're [the residents] not anchored in the here and now. They no longer read newspapers; they sit and watch television or stare out the window. Here, they're anchored in the here and now, and look forward to next week." *Times Union*, January 4, 1982

fully fought these threatened changes and, instead of cutting back on the number of beds and services available to residents, applied to New York State for permission to expand even further.

expand their medical services and treat more people who needed more complex care. With the implementation of these federal and state programs came additional regulations and oversight.

Complying with the new regulations not only meant keeping a meticulously good facility, but also involved welcoming people of all faiths to abide by the new "non-discriminatory" conditions imposed by the federal government. In practical terms, this meant that the Home could continue to be Jewish in its orientation and kosher in its cooking. But it would accept a small number of people from other faiths and ethnic backgrounds who applied for admittance.

The Home also had to fight impending legislation in the mid-1970s that threatened to transfer Jewish patients to other institutions that were less expensive but where they would not be in supportive religious environments so important to many in their later years. The Home success-

I Remember

Harriet Lewis recalls her work as director of volunteers and Auxiliary activist.

"In 1972, after other part-time jobs and grown children, I became director of volunteers at the Jewish Home. I served in that capacity for seven years—it was a wonderful experience and I came to feel very dedicated to the Home and the services it offered.

"I left the job in the summer of 1979, and about two months later was asked to be president of the Auxiliary. The first board meeting I conducted was the first one I had ever attended. In those days the volunteer director was asked to make a report at each board meeting, but did not participate in the business part of the meeting.

"During the two years I served we became fund-raisers for the Home—a task the Auxiliary had not undertaken actively for more than twenty years. The first year we re-activated the "1180 Club," which people could join for $10. At each Auxiliary general meeting, names were drawn and monies in the amount of $10, $20 and $50 were won by those people. Many of the winners contributed the money they won back to the Auxiliary. We made about $6,000 and thought it was a huge success!

"The next year we sponsored a "Gala" at George Eastman House. We had a film program at the Dryden, honored past presidents, enjoyed lovely refreshments and made about $1,800.

"I worked with wonderful women, many of whom had been volunteers at the Home when I first met them, made loyal friends, and continued to love working with and for the residents. Nothing is more satisfying!"

James K. Littwitz, Myron Silver, and Dr. William Feldman at a 1976 meeting.

New Horizons for Gray Panthers

Although many elderly in the community required infirmary care, scores of others in Rochester's Jewish community were enjoying life without serious illness. Despite the popular myth that most elderly people are institutionalized, the care for the elderly usually takes place in older people's own homes by family members, friends, and with the selective support of local social services. A cross-section of today's aged population reveals that less than 10 percent are in institutions at any one time. This proportion rises from about 3 percent of those aged 65 to 75 to 9 percent of those over 75 and to 20 percent of those over 85. Among the noninstitutionalized elderly, the amount of help needed varies greatly. Some are housebound and immobile; some can only go out with difficulty, while others are quite mobile but need companionship of their peers and supportive services.

In response to the needs of this growing population of seniors, the Home, under the leadership of president Mike Silver (1974-76) and with the assistance of an able Day Care Committee composed of Dr. William Feldman, Norman Trottenberg, Dr. Max Presberg, Ethel Kowal, Betty Oppenheimer and Shirley Axelrod, began developing outreach programs designed for people who wanted companionship and activities but who did not need full-time supervised care. This program, called New Horizons (1974), was the first of its kind in western New York and one of the first in the nation.

New Horizons is a social day program for older adults who become isolated because of health or other problems. It began meeting once a week, supervised by Paulette Zigelstein Geller, who became a national leader in adult day services, and in 1975 expanded to three times a week. This program provides an opportunity for socialization, nursing monitoring and social work outreach. Participants engage in all sorts of activities. These include a wide variety of guest lectures, discussion groups on political issues, crafts workshops, side trips to the Memorial Art Gallery and Dryden Theater at George Eastman House and a hot kosher lunch. It has enabled many seniors to continue to have a high quality of life. In 1997, the program had 55 participants. "Many people are isolated, depressed, and shouldn't be left alone," explained Louise P. Whitney, then director of Day Services. "New Horizons was designed to prevent the depression and other emotional problems that isolation can cause." As one 90-year-old participant recalled: "It is something to look forward to, a chance to get out and see other people."

For those individuals who require something more intensive and comprehensive but who still don't need residential care, the Home initiated the DayTimers program in 1981, a one- to six-day-a-week program for both the physically and mentally impaired. It offers social and intellectual experiences as well as a full health program and rehabilitative services. It provides transportation, nutritional counseling, help with personal hygiene and social work outreach. There is a very high staff to participant ratio in the program, which has as its goal to enhance participant independence and quality of life and allow them to stay home for as long as possible. In 1997, there were 113 participants.

To honor the memory of Dr. William Feldman (an early and active proponent of day

At the 50th anniversary celebration, from left to right are Garson Meyer, Leon Germanow, Ginni Nusbaum, Jacob Ark, Mort Nusbaum, Herbert Mock, and Betty Mock.

services), his wife, Marilyn, endowed an annual seminar, conducted by the Day Services department for professional staff and family members in the wider community, focusing on different aspects of day programming for the elderly. It is believed to be the only such seminar in the region dedicated to those who work in adult day services.

Greener Pastures

By 1980, there were 242 residents in the Home and 250 staff members. Over 85 percent of these residents were Medicaid recipients, and the list of applicants was growing. The need for more space was again paramount, but expanding in the St. Paul Street area was no longer viable or even desirable. Most Jews had moved away from Joseph Avenue to growing Jewish communities in the suburbs. Trips to the Home were often problematic for visitors, many of them well over sixty, and who didn't enjoy traveling to this downtown area. Urban blight and the inexorability of time had taken their toll. Even younger people found it inconvenient to drive downtown in the evenings or on the weekends, since most Jews now lived in Brighton, Irondequoit, Pittsford and other areas of Greater Rochester.

It was becoming increasingly clear to some within the leadership of the Home that St. Paul Street was not where the future would be and that it should relocate to an area that was more accessible and more suburban, preferably in Brighton, where the greatest number of Jewish families now lived. This was a difficult decision, and it was not shared by everyone. However, a new cadre of leaders, particularly people like Burton Tanenbaum, Emanuel Goldberg and Leon Germanow, successfully made the case for the move—conceptually, practically and financially. Serious conversations on the issue of relocation began during the tenure of president

1983

The Jewish Home begins campaign drive for Winton Road site construction.

Campaign cabinet named to raise the $5 million in private donations needed for Winton Road facility. Garson Meyer, Dr. Morris J. Shapiro, Emanuel Goldberg,

Fred B. Kravetz, Neil Norry, and Myron S. Silver are elected.

The Winton Road Jewish Home plans are approved by the federal government. DeWolff Partnership Inc. of Fairport designed the building. LeCesse Brothers Contracting Inc. will build it. Of the planned 362 beds, 188 will be designated for skilled

nursing care. "To make it a home for the residents, the rooms will be a pleasant size, with each resident having a window to look out of, even in the double rooms," Ruth Rosenberg says. There will be an expanded day care program, "to help keep people in their homes as long as possible." *Times Union*, May 17, 1983

Winton Road celebrates the site groundbreaking on June 27. The new Home is to house 362, and will cost $26 million.

Artist Sue Klein begins art classes for the residents.

Bonds for $24,055,000 are sold to finance the construction of the Winton Road facility.

An outbreak of intestinal flu cases prompts a restriction on visits to residents. About 50 residents and staff are affected.

The Central Conference of American Rabbis (Reform) votes to recognize as Jews —even without conversion—persons with one Jewish parent, father or mother, as long as they identify with the Jewish community.

I Remember

Nathalie and Emanuel Goldberg, former Auxiliary and Board presidents, remember their work for the Home from the 1960s through the 1980s.

"The Home has been an important, even central, part of our lives. We have never stopped being involved with it. Nathalie began her involvement first, working as a volunteer until she took on leadership responsibilities for the Auxiliary. I was asked to join the Board. For us, it was truly a collaborative effort.

"We recall thinking, planning and working very hard in the 1960s on the concept of a senior adult apartment complex connected to the Home. We felt strongly that this was a worthwhile project. For a variety of reasons, we could not get it done then. We are grateful that The Summit at Brighton is finally seeing our dream and the dreams of many others come to fruition, albeit in a different form.

"Mostly, we remember the wonderful, capable people we worked with, individuals like Dr. Eli A. Leven, Leon Germanow, Herbert F. Mock [the son-in-law of Samuel H. Greenhouse], Rose Wolfe, Beatrice Goran and Dr. Morris Shapiro. Rose was the quintessential volunteer—hardworking and always there, and Morrie was the ideal leader—tireless, sincere, dedicated, brilliant intellectually and a great communicator. The Home's most valuable natural resource is its people, and in that regard we are wealthy indeed."

Emanuel Goldberg (1971-73); planning was initiated by his successors, Mike Silver and Donald M. Cohn (1977-79), with assistance from Jim Littwitz and Burton Tanenbaum (1986-88). Silver stressed that the Home was entering a period of transition and change, but that "we should not lose our traditional heritage" in the process. In 1981, the Board, led by Ruth Rosenberg (the Home's first woman president), found and purchased 20 acres of grassy land on Winton Road for $400,000. When the plans for expansion were approved by the state and federal governments two years later, the DeWolff Partnership was retained to design the new building, which aimed to house 362 residents—each to have a window in their room. The project was supervised on the Board level by the "four horsemen," Burton Tanenbaum, William Feldman, Donald Cohn and Mike Silver, with Feldman, a Kodak physicist, responsible for the daily details of the project.

Raising money for the new building would be a real challenge, requiring millions of dollars and hours of devotion and expertise. The Board appointed Dr. Morris Shapiro, Fred Kravetz and Mike Silver to spearhead a $5 million capital campaign. Garson Meyer, Neil Norry, Emanuel Goldberg and Burton Tanenbaum were also asked to join the team as leaders. The community responded generously and with dispatch. Six million dollars was raised relatively quickly, well over the goal, as a testimony to the affection people felt for the Home. Hundreds of individuals contributed, including a number of outstanding and generous gifts in excess of $100,000 from people like William and Sheila Konar (Occupational Therapy), Isaac Gordon Foundation (Radiology), Harry Lippman (Board Room), Louis Wolk (ten rooms), Harry Achter (Pharmacy), Max Adler Foundation (Adult Day Care), Ames-Amzalek Fund (reception area), Ted Gordon Family Charity (lobby), Emanuel and Nathalie Goldberg (Activity Center), Jean and Ruben Natapow and family (grand-

Among those who attended the Jewish Home's Auxiliary dinner dance at the Rochester Plaza were, from left: Mildred Schrier, Marian Cohen, Ruth Shecket, Sheila Berghash, Helen Silver, Florence Phillips, Arlean Levinson and Shirley Axelrod.

Home Auxiliary Has Dinner Dance

The **Jewish Home and Infirmary's Ladies Auxiliary** held a dinner dance Sunday evening, May 20, in the Rochester Plaza Hotel, where more than $100,000 was pledged to the Building Fund.

More than 250 persons attended the event, which featured society orchestra leader Lester Lanin, who came from New York City to furnish the music.

A cocktail hour was followed by a formal candlelight dinner in the hotel's grand ballroom.

Proceeds will be used for the Craft Room and Gift Shop at the new Home on Winton Rd. S., Brighton, according to Sora Lee Goldberg and Shirley Axelrod, co-chairpersons of the dinner dance.

daughter of founder Brina Appelbaum) (library), Max Farash, Margaret and Herman Schwartz (Physical Therapy), the Daisy Marquis Jones Foundation (medical wing) and the Auxiliary ($100,000). It was the beginning of a new chapter for the Home.

On June 23, 1983, the groundbreaking took place as planned. The following year, president Dr. Martin Nacman and newly appointed chief executive officer Arnold S. Gissin, who came to the Home from the position of Rochester area director for the New York State Department of Health, oversaw the construction of the handsome

brick structure on Winton Road. The magnificent new facility was dedicated on June 2, 1985, as hundreds of loyal supporters attended. A week later, on June 9, under the coordination of Judy Lurie and Paulette Zigelstein Geller and the watchful eye of administrator Arnold Gissin, the residents moved in.

This was an incredible undertaking that required extensive planning. Everything went smoothly and without incident. Over 250 volunteers individually met the residents, packed them and moved them to the new facility. Jim Littwitz was the Board coordinator for this massive

enterprise. Linda Rubens, director of volunteers (1983-86), supervised. People arrived at 6:00 in the morning and worked until mid-afternoon. It was really a very exciting day in the community, one of those defining experiences that left everyone involved feeling enthusiastic and grateful. There were also over 100 tour guides headed by Helen Silver, Etta Atkin and Ethel Kowal, who ushered visitors through the new facility. It was a unique outpouring of community support and teamwork, one of the high points in the history of the Home, an example of *gemilut chesed* (acts of loving kindness) at its best. By three o'clock in the afternoon on June 9, all the residents were comfortably settled in their new rooms. A new era in care for the Jewish elderly in Rochester was to begin.

Judy Lurie receives recognition for decades of devoted service.

Life means little, if it be lived only for one's self; that the dignity of each human being is a treasure for all; that to extend a helping hand to those in need is as basic as our own food and shelter. "

1950 Board of Directors resolution for Lester Nusbaum

chapter four

From Winton Road to The Summit

"He who learns from

the elderly

is like one who

eats ripe grapes

and drinks aged wine."

The Ethics of the Fathers

1 9 8 5 - 1 9 9 8

Residents of the Home in the 1980s, from left to right, are Louis Carr, Ida Koren, Ruby Rabin, Charles Navis, Hyman Friedman, and Jewel Rothchild.

Reminiscence group led by Aviva Groskin in the 1980s.

"*When it comes to the Jewish Home, people put aside their differences. The Home comes first.*"

Arnold Gissin, president/CEO

I n 1985, the impressive new $25 million facility at 2021 Winton Road South opened, with a capacity for 362 residents. It took over ten years and the leadership of six presidents—Emanuel Goldberg, Mike Silver, Donald Cohn, Ruth Rosenberg, Dr. Martin Nacman and Burton Tanenbaum, the assistance of dedicated Auxiliary activists like Shirley Axelrod, Helen Silver (the late wife of Mike Silver), Enid Wallack, Harriet Lewis, Ruth Shechet and Mildred Schirer—to bring the new Home to life.

Groundbreaking ceremony in 1983 for the new facility on Winton Road. From left to right are Charles Gelb, *Ruth Shechet, Burton Tanenbaum, Ruth Rosenberg, Donald Cohn, and Rabbi Shaya Kilimnick.*

Moving into the new Home on June 9, 1985.

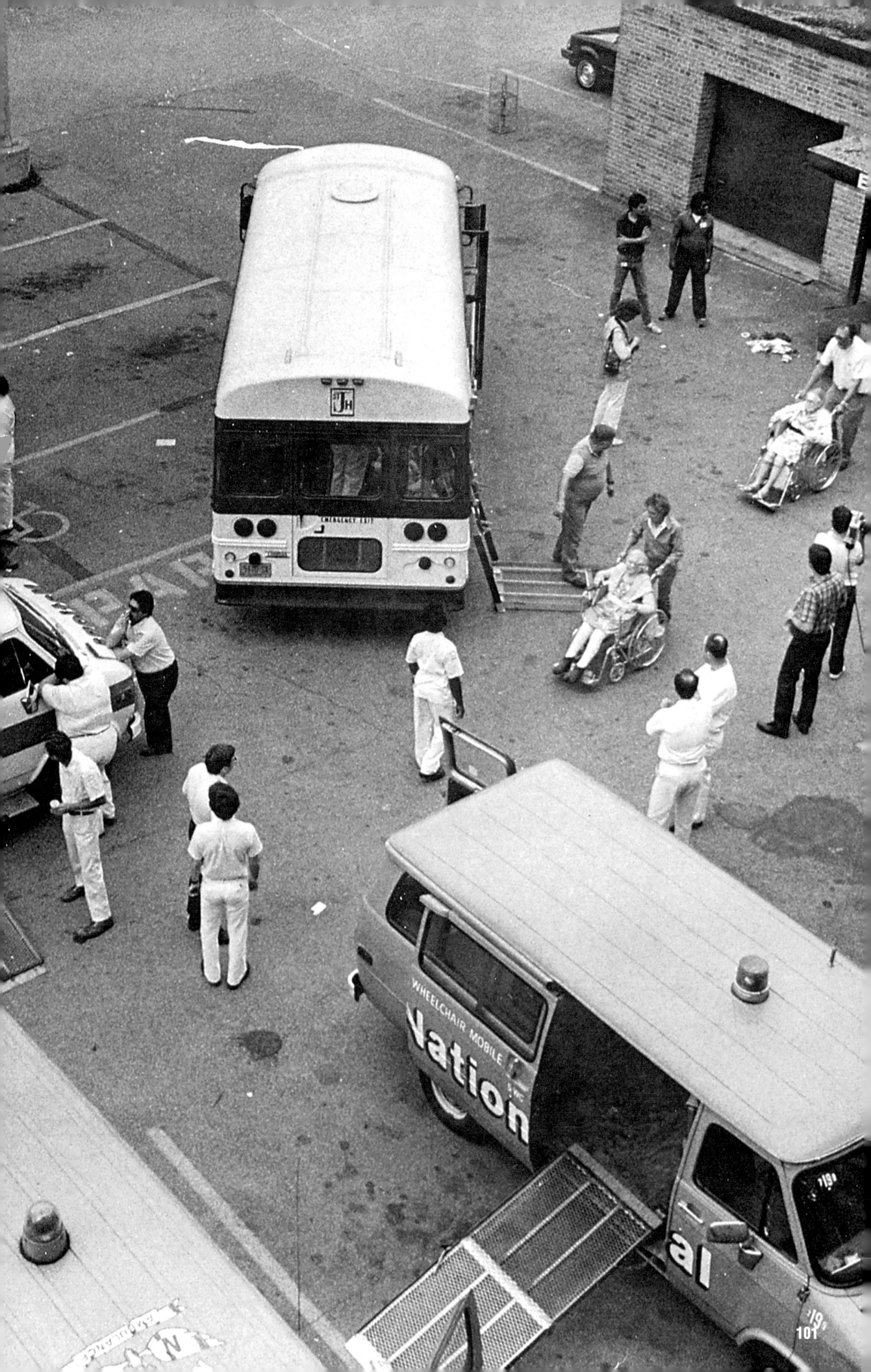

Moving the Torah scrolls from St. Paul Street into the new facility are Nathan Goldberg, Milton Karz, Arthur Blumenthal, and Lou Osband.

Karen Mitchell Democrat and Chronicle

Perry connecting beams at [Je]wish Home and Infirmary construction in Brighton.

Jewish home plans June move by caravan

By Craig Gordon
Democrat and Chronicle

As the new $26 million Jewish Home and Infirmary takes shape, administrators are making plans for a caravan of buses, vans and ambulances to move residents there next June.

The convoy will move an entire 242-bed nursing home — including residents, staff and equipment — from the current Jewish home at 1180 St. Paul St. to the new seven-story building at 2120 S. Winton Road in Brighton, just south of Interstate 590. Administrators hope to complete the move in one or two days.

Ground was broken for the new 362-bed facility in June 1983. It is set to open June 15, 1985. For a short time during the move, both the new and old homes will be operating.

"It's a tremendous undertaking, because all these things have to be fully operational during the move," said Baylee Green, director of community relations for the home. "There has to be staff in both places because not everyone is going to go out the door here and in the door there at the same time."

Home administrators began working on a plan to transfer residents four months ago, after studying similar moves made by other hospitals, said Arnold Gissin, assistant administrator. Industrial engineer Frank Reynolds of Eastman Kodak Co. has volunteered to help plot the trip.

One hospital called on the National Guard for help when it made a move to a new home, and the Jewish home might do the same, Green said.

An additional 155 full-time workers will be hired for the new facility before the move, Green said. The St. Paul Street home employs 260 people.

The staff is working to make the trip to new quarters as easy as possible for the residents. "They are going to be leaving very familiar surroundings, and there is some apprehension of the unknown," Green said.

After consulting with psychologists and other experts, administrators will decide the best way to execute the switch. Details include such minute points as whether residents should unpack themselves or have their new rooms fully set up for them when they arrive, Gissin said. Each of the rooms will have new beds and furniture.

"With an elderly population, change is even more difficult. We're sure they'll be very much prepared" by June, he said.

The St. Paul Street residents can follow the new project's progress by checking photographs and copies of plans on a bulletin board or by asking staffers, Gissin said. "When the residents hear about it, they're upbeat and excited."

The new home is being built because the St. Paul Street site has no room for expansion, and demand for nursing-home beds is increasing.

The new building will be shaped like a pinwheel, with wings extending from a central hub, called the centrum.

Administrative offices will be on the first floor. The centrum will contain service areas, lounges, recreation areas and a pharmacy.

Recreation areas will be built on the home's 20-acre plot. There also are plans to build a retirement home apartment complex on the land, but no date has been set for its construction, Gissin said.

The new home was financed through the sale of $21 million in 40-year tax [...] the [...] nan[...] mill[...]

Part of the crowd at the dedication ceremony on June 2, 1985. In the first row is Elizabeth Cohn. In the second row from left to right are Elizabeth Schwartz, Ella Oken, Shirley Bunis, and Helen Lavine.

Aerial view of the Winton Road facility.

The 1985 annual meeting. Standing from left to right are Mike Silver, Leon Germanow, Garson Meyer, Joe Silverstein, Dr. Eli Leven, Donald Cohn, and Dr. Martin Nacman.

Renamed the Jewish Home of Rochester, the six-story building boasts an enhanced and cheery Café Shalom located beside a spacious bank of windows on the "street of shops," where seniors can daily chat with friends and relatives over soda, coffee and snacks; a gift shop, where they can purchase sundries and relatives can buy all sorts of Judaica gifts; a beauty and barber shop for weekly shampoos, haircuts, manicures, pedicures and permanents; an impressive library; and a spacious and simply designed synagogue area nearby where *Shabbat* services and religious holidays are celebrated under the general supervision and guidance of Rabbi Shaya Kilimnick of Congregation Beth Shalom.

The Home is also beautified by the many original works of art that are carefully chosen by a committee chaired by Essie Germanow and displayed throughout the building. Many residents also have regular visits from foster grandchildren and students from the area's universities and high schools, who adopt seniors at the Home and take them for walks, help them write letters, bring them news from the world and, most of all,

Tea and cookies, a tradition at Café Shalom.

listen attentively to their dreams and memories. There are also over 300 volunteers who do incredible hands-on work with the residents— daily bingo, exercise classes, bridge, music, meaningful conversations and contact, as well as staffing the gift shop and the café. Since 1978, Aaron Braveman, the son of founding Board member Joshua Z. Braveman, has offered an Options for Jewish Learning course that has kept many residents abreast of Jewish issues and current events. Bob Weinberg donates a copy of one of his three books of poetry to each of the newly admitted residents. Bob and his wife, Adelaide, are also responsible for the annual strawberry festival and monthly happy hour.

Equally important, a dedicated and highly skilled staff of more than 500 full- and part-time doctors, nurses, certified nursing assistants, therapists, social workers and other professionals are on hand to take care of residents and make sure the Home operates as smoothly as possible.

Almost all residents these days were born in America, and some are from affluent families. About 100 are relatively self-sufficient and need only partial nursing care, but that number is declining as new admissions tend to be older and increasingly frail.

*Gift store display
at the Auxiliary
Gift Shop.*

and a warm and caring Jewish atmosphere. The remaining two-thirds of residents are critically ill and need round-the-clock nursing assistance. Many suffer from some form of dementia; they need help with everything from dressing in the morning to eating. There are also nineteen beds for people who need short-term rehabilitation and who stay from one to three months in the Weinberg-Manson Short-Term Rehabilitation Center and then return to their own homes.

Residents are drawn by the Home's congenial atmosphere and the opportunity to have companionship, stimulating programs, home-cooked meals

*Happy times at
the Jewish
Home.*

At Home

Philip Boslov

Artist in residence Lynne Feldman with residents Janet Holstein and Ida Rapp.

Bowling at the Home.

Three generations of the family of founder and first treasurer Frank Sherman.

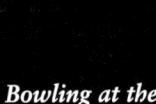

The Art Committee of the Jewish Home. Standing from left to right are Elmer Louis, Shelly Cresov, Seymour Merrall, *Penny Pinsky, and Sue Klein. Seated from left to right are Roz Goldman, Chairperson Essie Germanow, and Elizabeth Cohn.*

Staff Laugh Olympics.

The Residents Chorus.

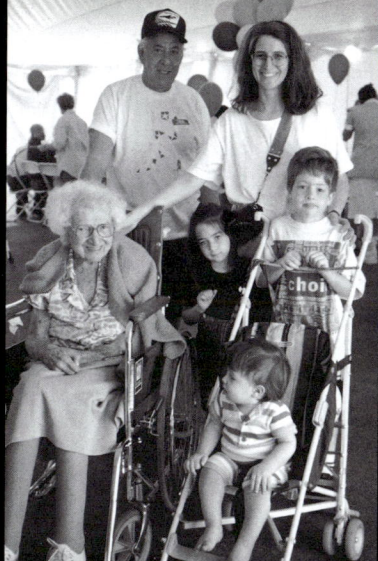

The family of Mrs. Julius Simon, granddaughter and great-grandchildren.

Volunteer manicurist Dorothy Pres with resident Sylvia Will.

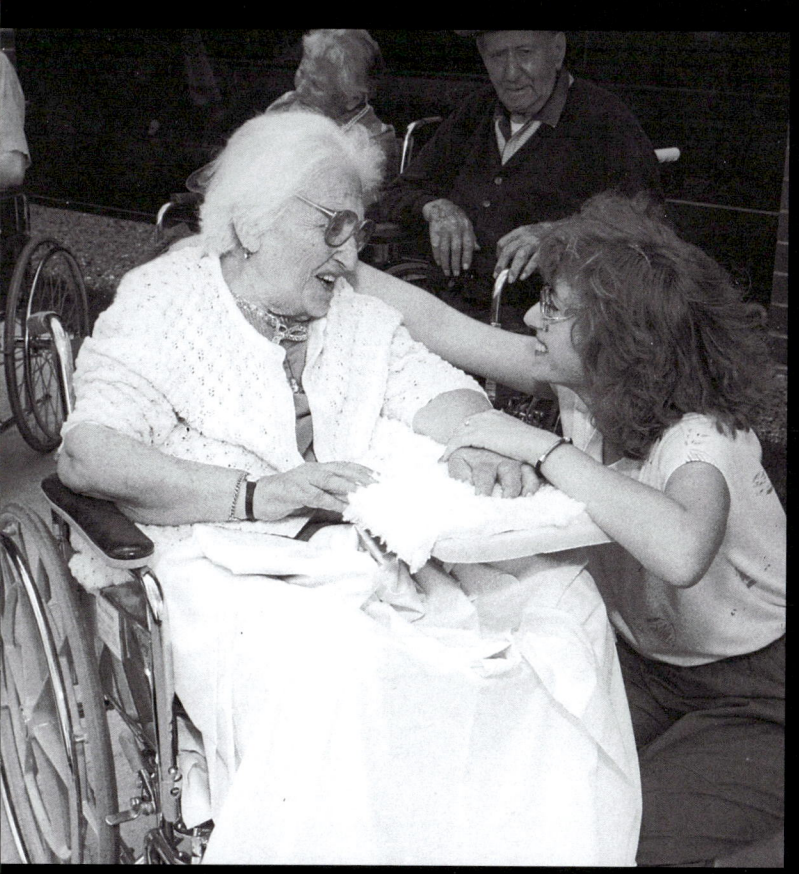

Sunshine Olympics.

1984

In February 1984, Arnold Gissin is appointed administrator of the Home.

1985

The new Home at 2021 Winton Road South opens with the capacity to house 362 residents and to serve 185 people in two day services. New name of the Home is Jewish Home of Rochester.

The Executive Committee agrees that "having evening meetings in the facility would add vibrancy and promote community awareness."

A Wilson Foundation grant enables the Home to begin an Alzheimer's Disease and Related Disorders program. At the time the grant is awarded, the Home's New Horizons and Communicare programs accept Alzheimer's patients.

Residents and staff continue to adjust to changes in the new building and work toward making it more homelike. A number of rooms are converted to resident lounges and supplied with comfortable furniture and televisions.

In an effort to reduce funding to nursing homes, New York State develops complex ways to categorize patients and determine payments for long-term care. The Home's move makes its Medicaid reimbursement arrangements with New York State more complicated and the budget comes up short.

Rochester places 15th of 329 cities in Rand McNally's *Places Rated Almanac*, which cites employment, housing prices, public safety, climate, culture, health care, and recreation as factors.

1986

The Café Shalom Cabaret began a tradition of regular performances for residents.

The Home reaches its total resident capacity of 362.

1986 continued

The Home dedicates the Arline and Fred B. Kravetz Pavilion, which is the North Wing of the Home. This wing includes Café Shalom, the Crafts Room, Barber/Beauty Shop, Therapeutic Recreation Department, Volunteer Department, Music Room and Library (first-floor area); second through sixth floors (60 rooms housing 98 residents), and ground level (laundry, housekeeping, and receiving offices). Presented by Mr. Kravetz in honor of his wife, it was one of the largest single gifts to the Jewish Home.

Florence Phillips, president of the Auxiliary, reports that 230 people attended its fashion show. Funds from Auxiliary projects like these allow Café Shalom to be available seven days a week at no cost to residents, support the Gift Shop, and provide for outings for residents.

An apartment committee, headed by Myron Silver, begins to investigate a building project for seniors that would one day become The Summit—a life care retirement community sponsored by the Jewish Home.

The Home hosts the Sunshine Olympics in conjunction with area nursing homes.

Dr. Bernard Shore becomes the Home's new medical director.

The New Horizons program is running at capacity and has a waiting list of 20. The Community Programming Committee, led by B. Oppenheimer, investigates satellite programs.

The American Association of Homes for the Aging recognized the Wilson program for individuals with Alzheimer's disease as "Innovative Program of the Year."

1987

The Home mourns the loss of Joseph E. Silverstein, who led Sabbath and holiday services at the Home for 65 years.

The Home spends $33,900 to update its computer system to handle clinical as well as financial systems. According to Arnold Gissin, "A definite need exists for data processing systems to improve efficiency in nursing, to reduce errors and to have retrievable data to manage under RUGS [Medicaid's classification for reimbursement]."

The Home's Guidelines for Care allow residents to choose the type of care they would want "in the final stages of life."

Farewell luncheon in 1988 for John Lovenheim (right), Foundation president in 1986 and 1987.

Ed Bloom, Linda Rubens, and Etta Atkin at a 1994 Golden Alliance function.

Coping with Financial Crisis

While Medicaid, a government program, subsidizes about 85 percent of the residents in the Home, this revenue falls far short of covering the cost of operating a quality facility. The battle to retain governmental support has been intense. Each year, despite rising costs, the Medicaid reimbursement falls farther behind in meeting the costs of providing care.

It was evident that with the changes in government reimbursement, the Home would need supplementary revenue sources to help the Home cover deficits necessary to continue to provide the high quality of care it has always been known for. To help address this shortfall and to provide for the financial health of the Home, the Jewish Home Foundation was re-energized by Donald Cohn in 1985. He asked John Lovenheim to get involved. Lovenheim, who took over as president of the Foundation in 1986, with the assistance of Helen Silver, was instrumental in setting it up on a professional footing. Linda Rubens was hired as a full-time director of development, the office was organized, records were computerized, committees were set up, and other outstanding leaders were brought on board, including Edward Bloom, the current

Foundation president and
grandson and son of past
Home Board members Samuel
H. Bloom and Seymour
Bloom, respectively.

In 1988, the Foundation
established a Golden Alliance
annual giving program. It was
really the dream of Fred
Kravetz, Mike Silver and Dr.
Morris Shapiro to have an
annual giving program, and it
has turned out to be one of
the most successful initiatives
the Foundation took. The
Golden Alliance has energized
and activated hundreds of
people, who have become

supporters and leaders of the
Home as well as annual
contributors. The outpouring
of support has been phenom-
enal, a tribute to the deep
affections that people in the
Jewish community feel for the
Home. "This Home belongs
to the Jewish community and
the needs are great," Bloom
notes. The Foundation, with
Golden Alliance assistance,
makes it possible for the
Home to deliver the quality of
care that the Jewish community expects and deserves,
without regard for ability to
pay. It supports Jewish religious services, Passover seders,
lectures, cultural programs
and entertainment that cannot
be covered by the operating
budget. It has helped keep the
Home a home. People's
interest in the Home was
intensified through their
annual giving experiences, and
this certainly led to the establishment of a number of
endowed funds that have
enhanced the lives of the resi-

dents. These include the
Minnie Cohen Arts and Entertainment Series, established by
Lillian Atkins and Erwin
Atkins in memory of Lillian's
mother and Erwin's grand-
mother, Minnie Cohen; the
Hirschland Fund, established
by Janet and Henry Hirschland to support continuing
nursing education for staff;
and the Arthur and Louise
Wasserman Employee and
Nursing Recognition Funds.

Other important lay
leaders who have been key to
the success of the Golden
Alliance include Etta Atkin,
Marilyn Frank, Essie
Germanow, Sheila Markin,
Irving Mann, Dr. Morris
Shapiro, Fred Kravetz, Mike
Silver, Phyllis Mindell, Elizabeth Schwartz, Carolyn Miller,
and, of course, Linda Rubens.
It is, in fact, her enthusiasm,
dedication, personality, and
boundless energy that has
helped ensure the success of
these programs. She has
served as the "ambassador" of
the Jewish Home in the
community.

Midway through its first
year of operation, the Alliance
raised over $130,000 in
support. By 1990, it had 325
members, who provided
$250,000 a year in annual
giving. In 1997, it had over
540 members and raised
almost $400,000.

*Mike Silver,   Louis S. Wolk at
Fred Silverstein,   a Golden Alliance
William Green-   dinner in 1993.
berg, and*

1987 continued
The waiting list for admission to the Home steadily increases.

Following a growing trend among businesses and nonprofits, a Board committee prepares a long-range plan with two- and four-year objectives.

Debbie Ullian joins the staff as the Home's first physician assistant.

The Home begins a "Pay for Performance Merit System" for employees.

A shortage around the country of registered nurses and nurses' aides affects nursing homes, who must compete with higher-

paying hospitals. Some homes even begin recruiting in English-speaking countries such as Scotland and Ireland. According to a report by Arnold Gissin, "The impact of the nursing crunch is hitting the JHR in a way never felt before."

Linda Rubens, the Home's first director of development, spearheads an annual giving program.

The Home has 754 paid members. Volunteers provided 27,000 hours of service.

1988
Garson Meyer, president of the Jewish Home of Rochester from 1943 to 1952, and a long-time friend of the aging, died at the Home after a long illness.

Under the leadership of Fred Kravetz, Mike Silver and Dr. Morris Shapiro, the Golden

Alliance, a membership organization of high-level supporters, forms with 200 members.

RUGS, the state's reimbursement program that pays higher rates to care for certain types of patients (those who are bedridden or who must be fed intravenously), continues to create losses because many of the Home's

Health Care Challenges of the 90s

There were also important structural and governmental changes that the Home had to deal with in this period. Prompted by the massive rise in nursing home costs, New York State's economic downturn of the early 1990s, and the growing population of frail elderly people suffering from dementia and needing full-time care, the following rigorous governmental intervention was set in motion.

Under a totally revised Medicaid reimbursement system entitled RUGS (Resource Utilization Groupings), nursing homes were placed in the position of giving priority to applicants whom New York State considered critically ill with physical ailments. Usually, these residents needed complex care and were often completely bedridden. Of importance to the Home was the growing number of Jewish elderly people suffering from Alzheimer's and other forms of dementia who were not considered critically ill under RUGS but who still required

significant services to meet their needs. For these residents, Medicaid reimbursement was far below the cost of providing the care, even though the individuals could not live on their own, and their care was beyond what family members could provide.

The Home, despite the financial consequence, continued—and still continues—to admit those with dementia even if they exhibit significant behavioral problems. In the late 1980s and early 1990s, the Home lost hundreds of thousands of dollars annually primarily due to its willingness to admit people with dementia regardless of the reimbursement implications and also by not giving priority to private-paying applicants at the expense of those on Medicaid. The Home has always been primarily concerned with serving those most in need, and it continues that commitment.

During this period, the Home was also experiencing trouble recruiting and retaining nurses and aides, in part because it was unable to

The ice storm of 1991 created hardship for the Home and challenged a caring staff.

residents fall into low-reimbursement categories. The Home considers slowing down admissions of lower level RUGS residents and admit more non-Jewish people to increase the case mix, but instead decides to increase fund-raising efforts.

A flu epidemic hits Monroe County. Residents at the Home take part in a University of Rochester drug study.

Essie Germanow, who is responsible for selecting art for exhibition at the Home, secures a grant from Arts for Greater Rochester for local artist Lynne Feldman to create a painting for the Home. Residents watch and comment to the artist as she works.

Under the guidance of Dr. Bernard Shore, the Home establishes a relationship with the University of Rochester's School of Medicine and moves toward its goal of becoming a geriatric teaching center.

Nurses at the Home receive a substantial raise to help reduce high turnover, a problem faced by nursing homes across the country.

The Home's budget now runs about $12 million a year.

The Home loses more than $400,000 in Medicaid support because of RUGS.

Work begins on "Helen's Garden," an outside area large enough for 150 residents. Myron Silver donates and heads the project, which honors his wife, a longtime volunteer at the Home.

offer competitive salaries. "We had vacant positions and high staff turnover and used an enormous amount of temporary agency staff," recalls Arnold Gissin, "but we eventually, through pay adjustments and making the Home a premier place to work, managed to recruit and retain a wonderful staff. This organization was unmatched in the mid-1980s when it came to caring, but we didn't present ourselves adequately, we did not present the 'crisp' image our constituents wanted. At the same time, we were still perceived as leaders by our community and they supported us when asked."

In 1985, the Home began a funding relationship with the Jewish Community Federation. The Federation has been an annual supporter of the Home ever since. The grants from the Federation as well as periodic support from the Foundation for the Jewish Community to start up programs of a specific nature have helped the Home during

times of severe Medicaid reimbursement cutbacks. The Jewish Community Federation continues to support programs that help the Home maintain its uniquely Jewish programming and ambiance. Arnold Gissin remarked, "For all involved, the Home comes

first. This place is as mission-focused as any I've ever seen."

Medical director Dr. Bernard Shore.

I Remember

Aaron Braveman, the former educational director at Temple B'rith Kodesh, remembers his volunteer work at the Home.

"My involvement with the Jewish Home began in the mid-1970s. I came to the conclusion that it was important that learning continue, even well into old age. I proposed to the executive director, Will Greenberg, that something educational on an ongoing basis should be provided for the residents. The Home does wonderful things for the physical and social requirements of the residents; it has to meet their intellectual and Jewish needs as well.

"A committee was formed and Paulette Zigelstein Geller was very instrumental in this. I have been involved ever since. I lead a weekly group called Options for Jewish Learning that discusses issues of Jewish concern. Some of the residents are very alert and engaged, others come and just listen. The thing that I find most rewarding is trying to keep the residents active and intellectually vital. In the Jewish tradition, learning is a lifelong enterprise."

The Arline and Fred B. Kravetz Pavilion.

Arline and Fred Kravetz at the dedication of the Pavilion.

Dedication of Helen's Garden.

The Spirit of Support

While thousands of people contributed significantly to the new Home throughout this challenging period, giving gifts ranging from $25 to $100,000 and donating hours and hours of their time and skill, several specific contributions cannot be overlooked. These include:

Arline and Fred B. Kravetz Pavilion

In 1986, Fred Kravetz donated more than $500,000 in honor of his wife's recovery from a long illness. In recognition of his commitment and generosity, the Home named a special area in the North Wing as the Arline and Fred B. Kravetz Pavilion. Fred Kravetz was a leader and significant volunteer in every way, donating not only money, but time as well. He was instrumental in the move to Winton Road and was a force in the planning, fund-raising and setting the stage for The Summit at Brighton Retirement Community, an impressive residential facility opening in 1998 adjacent to the Home. "Fred's commitment to the Home was total—almost like a parent's love for a child. It was unconditional," remarked Edward Bloom at Fred Kravetz's death in 1993.

Helen's Garden

In 1988, Helen Silver's family honored her memory and years of undaunted volunteerism by landscaping a 15,000-square-foot garden with eloquent foliage, flowers, shrubs and a small pool. Called "Helen's Garden," the space is a welcome harbor for residents, who now have a beautiful place in which to walk freely and safely, experi-

Bessie Spector at the dedication of the Dr. Louis and Bessie Spector Medical Administrative Center.

Elie and Mildred Sokol.

The Mildred and Elie Sokol Porch and Pavilion.

Helen Silver.

Miriam Atkin, Etta Atkin, and Lillian Atkins.

The brick relief wall for the Atkin Center.

encing a new level of independence and dignity. "My mother believed in living life to its fullest," commented Helen's son, Rafi, at the dedication. "We wanted something that was not only beautiful, but spoke of her life as well. And the garden is exactly that. As a living memorial, the garden will bring pleasure and enjoyment to our residents. And that's what my mother always wanted for them."

Atkin Center

In 1994, the Atkin wives, Etta Atkin, Lillian Atkins, and Miriam Atkin, made a very generous gift to support adult day services. The Home recognized this gift by naming a 12,500-square-foot center as the Atkin Center in memory of their husbands, Morris, Sol and Samuel, who were brothers. These three women have been extraordinarily generous and helpful. Featuring a spacious central gathering room with a three-story-high ceiling, small seating clusters, activity areas, a walled-in terraced garden and a glass-enclosed walkway, the addition is now used for the DayTimers program, which was able to triple the number of participants from 37 to 113. "Our gift enables us to continue our husbands' commitment to family and to the community and enables the Home to provide the best care possible for our elderly," said the Atkin women. The unique sculptured inscription on the dedication wall appropriately reads: "The sheltering trees intertwined, nurtured by the soul of tradition." To further enhance the facility, Estelle B. Goldman, wife of M. Harry Goldman, a leader in the 1940s and 1950s, donated a garden for the Atkin Center.

The Brodsky family at the dedication of the Sara and Morton Brodsky Family Administrative Pavilion.

Lloyd Frank, Bea Silverstein Frank, and their son Fred at the dedication of the Joseph E. Silverstein Memorial Court.

Eva and Benjamin Lipson Walkway

Eva W. Lipson gave a major gift in memory of her husband, Benjamin. Benjamin Lipson's father, Eli, was the *shammes* (religious functionary) in the St. Paul Street synagogue of the original Home.

Dr. Louis and Bessie Spector Medical Administration and Educational Center

Bessie Spector gave the new medical wing in memory of her husband, Dr. Louis Spector, who had a distinguished career as a physician in the St. Paul Street area.

Weinberg-Manson Rehabilitation Center

To honor the memory and generosity of the late Harry and Jeanette Weinberg and Morton Manson, the Home named its new short-term rehabilitation center after them. The center provides short-term comprehensive rehabilitation services to assist patients, after they leave the hospital, to rebuild their strength and capabilities before going home. The Weinberg Foundation and Morton Manson made generous gifts to the Home. Manson's grandfather had been involved with the Home in its early years, and Morton Manson lived at the Home for three years prior to his death.

Mildred and Eli Sokol Porch and Solarium

The gift was made by Mildred and Eli Sokol in honor of the spirit of the Jewish Home, which has been a part of their families' lives since they were children. Eli Sokol's mother was a former resident of the original Home on St. Paul Street. Mrs. Sokol, a dancer, would often perform for the residents of the original Home.

Sara and Morton Brodsky Family Administrative Pavilion

Sara Brodsky, together with her children, made a major gift from their family foundation to help enhance the well-being of the Jewish elderly. Morton Brodsky, a former Board member, worked hard for the construction of the new Home.

Restraint Free

The Home not only continued to be a leader in forging ahead with new programs and facilities, aided by this spirit of support, but also became a pioneer in the movement to free nursing home residents from physical restraints. In the early 1970s, almost half of all the Home's residents were restrained in wheelchairs, chairs or beds in an attempt to keep them from falling and sustaining injury. This percentage reflected the practice in nursing homes throughout the nation. While restraint use was motivated by resident safety and perhaps to some small degree by short staffing, it was viewed by many as a necessary evil where the result was often debilitating, causing elderly people

1988 continued
The Auxiliary sponsors an oral history project that includes interviews with many female residents.

The Home pioneers restraint-free care in New York State. The State Department of Health provides a $156,000 grant to fund a two-year demonstration project.

The Golden Alliance has 245 members by year end.

1989
Private pay percentages continue to decrease at the Home and other nursing homes around the country.

The nursing shortage continues. The Home again strains its budget to raise salaries to compete for the best professionals. By mid year, New York State realizes the crisis the nursing shortage has caused for nursing homes and provides a "nurse wage reimbursement increase."

The Home improves its psychiatric services by adding a psychiatrist and making more nursing time available.

The Medicare Catastrophic Act brings an increase in funding to the Home.

Janet and Henry Hirschland establish a scholarship fund for staff members of the Home who wish to further their nursing education.

New Horizons expands and begins meeting at Temple B'rith Kodesh. Communicare expands its services to five days a week.

The Home conducts a survey and finds that "pleasant environment," "positive resident/staff interaction," "physical safety and comfort," and "respectful treatment" top the list as the most important factors in quality of life. The survey shows a high rate of satisfaction with the Home.

Arnold Gissin receiving the Lawrence A. Larson Award from the New York Association of Homes and Services for the Aging.

to become even more infirm and less mobile.

In 1988 the Home, under the leadership of Arnold Gissin and the professional guidance of medical director Dr. Bernard Shore, director of social work Rafi Silver and head nurse manager Nora Vrooman, became one of the few (perhaps five or six) nursing facilities in North America that decided to challenge this universally accepted practice. After much planning and study, the Home received a $156,000 grant from New York State to fund a two-year project that would reduce the use of restraints in treating the elderly.

I Remember

Elaine Kellmanson, vice president of the Jewish Home Foundation and wife of former Home president Joel Kellmanson, reflects on her reasons for becoming active in the Home.

"I took care of my family, I was active in our business and I was on the Compeer Board. Somewhere I realized I wasn't doing anything Jewish to give back to my community. I first started working on the Golden Alliance annual dinner. From that experience I was asked to be on the Foundation Board. Of all the Jewish organizations, the Jewish Home is like motherhood and apple pie. No one can say anything negative about it because it is so needed and because it holds a place of respect in the community. I also got involved because Fred Kravetz said that I should. One did not say no to Fred.

"What makes the Jewish Home unique is that everyone can come to the Home regardless of financial status. Because government reimbursement does not meet the needs, the Foundation makes up for the difference and makes it possible for everyone to benefit from the Home and its high level of care. There are many challenges we face for the future. Preserving its Jewish character and encompassing a wider mix of what Judaism represents in the United States are issues for me. I think we need to get the younger generation involved and find ways to make the Home not only a place for the elderly but a resource for the community to use, a focal point of community activity. The Summit at Brighton should help in that endeavor.

"Joel and I have had great fun working for an organization in two different 'divisions,' yet having a common focus."

The local press starts reporting on the success of the Home's restraint-free care. According to federal surveys, one article notes "about 41 percent of all nursing home residents were put in restraints this year, up from 25 percent in 1977." *Democrat and Chronicle,* 28 December 1989

1990
The children and grandchildren of Ruth and Moses Capell dedicate the volunteer workroom to the Home in honor of the Capells' 50th anniversary.

The Apartment Committee continues to shape The Summit project.

The Home sponsors a fundraising event in conjunction with the Rochester Philharmonic Orchestra—"An Evening with Jackie Mason."

The Do Not Resuscitate order and other life and death decisions continue to be controversial in the Jewish community. Arnold Gissin reports on a presentation at the North American Association of Jewish Homes and Housing for the Aged. A rabbi there says, "If you entrust a government with life and death decisions, you are then dependent on the ethics of the particular government who happens to be in power at the time."

The Home dedicates the Joseph E. Temkin Centrum at its 70th anniversary celebration.

The Board gives Elizabeth Schwartz a Special Recognition Award for her years of devoted service.

The Joseph E. Silverstein Memorial Court opens.

Membership at the Home nears 1,000.

Golden Alliance

*Golden Alliance
events and
committees.*

I Remember

Florence Phillips, former president of the Auxiliary (1987-88), captures the following memories of her involvement with the Home and its residents.

"I have early memories of my mother volunteering at the old Home on St. Paul Street. She used to go in several times a week to help feed the residents, change the sheets and do whatever was needed. I guess the ethic of taking care of others was instilled in me at a very early age.

"When my mother-in-law became a resident of the Home, I became more active. I worked in the crafts department, helping the residents sew aprons. I gradually took on added responsibility in the Auxiliary, volunteering in Café Shalom, heading up fund-raising and the like.

"The highlight of all of my activities was working with the residents. In the early 1990s, my husband and I took some of them to Strong Museum. It was gratifying to see how so many of them responded to the artifacts contained in the exhibits. These were items out of their histories as well.

"I grew very close to one of the residents, Molly Rossberg. I used to visit her often, sit together in the Café and talk about our families and especially her past. We talked a lot about Jewish women, about our mothers and grandmothers, about what it was like working as a young girl at Forman's. When I talked to her it was like talking to my grandmother; it was like opening a window into my past. Molly was an extraordinary woman who had great memories and stories.

"When middle-aged or young people think about the elderly, they inevitably compare their situations to their own. Then, aging is seen only as a series of losses—freedom, relationships, strength, beauty and future. We are rarely presented the views of older people about themselves and given an opportunity to hear how aging is experienced by them. I learned so much from Molly and the other residents I worked with. I learned that they had rich and beautiful personalities and still had so much to offer, to teach, to live. I feel so blessed that I have had these opportunities and that I have been involved in making life more comfortable and interesting for the residents."

1990 continued

Helen Gordon, president of the Auxiliary, announces that the group's major focus is resident quality of life. The Auxiliary begins putting a photograph and brief biography on the door of each resident's room.

Once again, the Home must adjust operations to government regulations as the Omnibus Budget Reconciliation Act of 1987 takes effect. The act adds many additional costs to the budget as well as changes in procedures.

A survey shows that the cost to operate Jewish nursing homes is much higher than for-profit counterparts. Costs range from $78 to $192 a day for Jewish homes, and $65 to $128 for for-profit homes. Reasons for this include: maintaining a kosher kitchen, providing religious services and more specialty foods for Jewish holidays, and hiring additional personnel to respond to the community, such as rabbis and committee liaisons.

The Home's medical staff attempts to help residents reduce unnecessary medications.

The Golden Alliance has 325 members, who provide a total of $250,000 in annual giving.

1991

Nursing homes across the country begin to feel the effect of shrinking government support and the general economic slowdown. Governor Mario Cuomo proposes drastic Medicaid cuts.

The Home joins with the New York Association of Homes and Services for the Aging in a campaign to fight Medicaid cutbacks, which will reduce the Home's budget by $700,000 in 1992.

The Home has nearly 300 volunteers. Twenty University of Rochester students participate in an adopt-a-grandparent program.

A community prayer service held at Temple Beth El for the Gulf War crisis draws over 1,400 people.

The Home receives a grant to become part of a study to work with voice-activated computerization (VAC).

A dramatic ice storm hits Rochester, leaving more than 200,000 RG&E customers powerless for up to two weeks. At the Home, the electricity was knocked out and the emergency generator ran for 52 hours, supporting heat, food service, and lighting. The night shift stays over, and staff from all departments pitches in to care for residents.

The worst recession in 10 years plagues Rochester and the nation.

The Home wins the Jewish Community Federation's Annual Elmer Louis Award for its Restraint Free Care program.

The Home becomes the first in the area to provide hospice care. Genesee Region Home Care is a partner in the program.

Ada Azoda, a native of Nigeria, forms a Thursday morning poetry group for residents.

Dr. Bernard Shore publishes article, on "Reducing Nursing Home Restraints," in the Fall 1991 *Contemporary Senior Health*.

1992
The residents build a dollhouse under the guidance of volunteer Dr. Jacqueline Braverman and raffle it at the Home to help the Jewish elderly hurt by the devastation of Hurricane Andrew.

The Home holds an "Evening with the Stars" dinner to honor Fred Kravetz, Dr. Morris Shapiro, and Myron Silver for their fundraising efforts and devoted service.

The New Horizons program moves back to the Home from Temple B'rith Kodesh; Communicare expands to six days of service.

QV 2021, a Total Quality Management (TQM) training program, begins at the Home. Arnold Gissin tells the Board that TQM is partly responsible for a 39 percent drop in the rate of staff turnover, 80 percent less agency use, improved staff morale, new enthusiasm, and fewer resident and family complaints.

The Home draws on recent Russian immigrants for staffing needs.

A detailed article about the Home's Restraint Free Care program appears in *Journal of Gerontological Nursing*.

Communicare has extended its hours to include Saturdays. The Home is the first nursing home in the area to offer adult day care weekend programs. *Home Highlights*, March 1992

Nora Vrooman, R.N., head nurse manager, publishes an article, "Releasing Restraints in the Nursing Home: It Can Be Done," in *Gerontological Nursing*.

1993
Louis Wolk becomes the first recipient of an honorary appointment to the Board of Governors at the Home's annual meeting.

The Jewish Home at 1180 St. Paul is razed.

"Restraints, used in nursing homes nationwide to protect residents from injury, are universally disliked by residents, families, staff, visitors and health care regulators," explained Arnold Gissin. "They are perceived as an assault on a resident's dignity as well as on their physical and emotional well-being. Staff searched for alternatives, for instance, using bed alarms with a buzzer to alert staff when someone was attempting to get out of bed or by placing gym pads on bedroom floors for residents who are at risk of falling during the night."

When the project began, the 49 percent of the Home's residents requiring skilled nursing care were restrained. When the program ended in 1990, less than one percent (two residents) were restrained and only for a short period when care was being provided. The Home subsequently won the Elmer Louis Award from the Jewish Community Federation for its program. Equally important, it became a model for all other nursing homes nationwide, many of whom adopted similar restraint-free policies. The Home takes pride in not only "untying" its own residents but influencing other nursing facilities locally, statewide and nationwide.

More Walkers Than Wheelchairs

The Home's second adult day care program, DayTimers (originally called Communicare) operates out of the Atkin Center and offers more intensive daily care for adults who need physical as well as emotional assistance. Like many other adult day care programs, its services provide equally important support for the spouses and families who need relief to carry on their daily routines.

When Josephine Drexel's husband, Howard, suffered a stroke several years ago, it would often take her two hours just to bathe, shave and dress him in the morning. "It was tiring," said the 75-year-old woman. "I'd get Howard all ready and have no energy left for myself."

When the couple enrolled in DayTimers' Early Bird Service at the Atkin Center, all that changed. After being picked up in the morning by the Early Bird bus, the couple would arrive in the Home. Aides would bathe, shave and dress Howard and then serve both Drexels breakfast and get Howard ready for the day's activities. Mr. Drexel now attends DayTimers six days a week and Josephine joins him on four of those days. It is this type of assistance that allows families to continue to support loved ones to remain living in the community and prevent premature admission to nursing homes.

In 1986, a new dimension was initiated for individuals with varying degrees of dementia. Financed with a $50,000 grant from the Joseph and Marie Wilson Foundation, the program was one of the first in the country to focus exclusively on people afflicted with Alzheimer's and other related disorders. "The Home has always excelled in meeting the needs of the community's elderly," said Burton D. Tanenbaum, then president of the Home. "It pioneered adult day care programs in Monroe County with New Horizons, and the need for additional programs has been identified locally and nationally."

Dementia Care

In 1997, a new dementia unit for residents opened, consisting of 38 beds and designed to give residents suffering from dementia more choice and control over their daily routine. As an example, if a resident wants to take a bath at midnight, a staff member accommodates him or her instead of imposing a fixed bathing schedule. "The unit represents a change in how care is delivered," explains Carol Maskiell, director of quality of life services. "We are moving away from the traditional concept of 'routines of care,' and toward a responsive care that changes as needed on a day-to-day or even hour-to-hour basis. To become more effective, staff members learn

Jewish Home Foundation leaders. Standing from left to right are Julian Gordon, John Lovenheim, Etta Atkin, and Ed Bloom. Seated is Elaine Kellmanson.

by experiencing how it feels to be dependent on others for care. Such training provides staff insight on why residents respond to caregiving in the way they do."

Congratulations to Mike Silver upon receiving the Trustee of the Year Award from the New York Association of Homes and Services for the Aging.

1993 continued

Rochester is singled out during the Clinton campaign for its excellent health care. Arnold Gissin and Congresswoman Louise Slaughter go to Washington, D.C., to meet with President Bill Clinton's transition team about issues concerning health care for the elderly.

The Home refinances its mortgage after many months of hard work and the assistance of Assemblyman Joseph Morelle.

The Auxiliary sponsors Bridges and Boundaries, an exhibit at the Strong Museum exploring the relationship of Jews and African Americans.

The Home gets a new logo.

According to the Home's medical director's report, "Residents admitted to the Home have increasingly been more frail, more often terminal, and also more demented or psychiatrically impaired....The character of nursing home residents is changing."

Department of Health surveyors leave the Home a day early, saying, "We couldn't find anything!" Comments include, "The nursing assistants are doing a good job," "Staff throughout the facility are very responsive," "Good sense of team," and "Residents have an incredible amount of freedom."

The Home has 1,500 members and 400 Golden Alliance members.

Board member Fred Kravetz dies. A resolution acknowledges his contributions, including co-chairing the building fund for the Winton Road facility and co-founding the Golden Alliance.

1994

The Home hires Sear Brown Engineers to help plan use of the 54 acres directly behind it. The Home purchases the land, including five lots, from Rochester Institute of Technology, in anticipation of building The Summit.

The name of the Communicare adult day care program is changed to "DayTimers."

The Home provides kosher meals for the Meals on Wheels program.

The Home dedicates the Atkin Center building, a 12,500-square-foot area for adult day care. The Center allows the Home to expand its DayTimers adult day health services from 37 to 65 participants a day.

The Weinberg-Manson Rehabilitation Center, an eight-bed nursing unit designed for older adults needing short-term, inpatient rehabilitation, opens at the Home.

75th Anniversary

Leon Germanow and Emanuel Goldberg.

PROCLAMATION

HONORING THE JEWISH HOME OF ROCHESTER
UPON THE OCCASION OF ITS SEVENTY-FIFTH ANNIVERSARY

WHEREAS, from its humble beginnings at 1162 St. Paul Street as the Jewish Home for the Aged, housing 10 residents, to its current facilities at 2021 Winton Road South, housing 362 residents, the Jewish Home of Rochester has served the Community of Monroe well over the past seventy-five years; and

WHEREAS, the Jewish Home of Rochester maintains, in-house, for the benefit of its residents, occupational and physical therapy facilities, adult day health services, a rehabilitation center, a pharmacology center, an opthalmology center, provides psychiatry services, an audiology department, podiatry services, radiology services and dentistry services; and

WHEREAS, the Jewish Home of Rochester has provided over the past seventy-five years, a place where members of the Jewish faith could live and celebrate their faith together while at a place where their medical and social needs could be met; and now, therefore, be it

RESOLVED, that we, New York State Senator Richard A. Dollinger and Assemblyman Joseph D. Morelle, congratulate the Jewish Home of Rochester upon their seventy-fifth anniversary of service; and be it further

RESOLVED, that a copy of this Proclamation be presented to Arnold S. Gissin, the President of the Jewish Home of Rochester on this 29th day of October, 1995.

Richard A. Dollinger
Senator - 54th District

Joseph D. Morelle
Assemblyman - 132nd District

Dated: October 29, 1995

I Remember

Mike Silver reflects on the life and contributions of Fred Kravetz.

"Fred was my mentor and dear friend. A character, a little rough around the edges, but extremely generous and gracious. Fred was a 'doer,' not a talker. He had an innate ability to cut through rhetoric and red tape and move on with the job. And he always delivered.

"Fred was a fantastic fund-raiser. Although he was a key leader of Federation, Israel Bonds, Temple B'rith Kodesh and the JCC, he focused his fabled tenacity and fund-raising passion for the Jewish Home with his pithy admonition to literally hundreds: 'If you don't like the Home, you don't like motherhood.' Some of his most effective fund-raising took place in the showers of the Irondequoit Country Club. It was hard to say no to him there or in other, less conspicuous environments.

"He also inspired others to serve the Home. His enthusiasm was contagious. If you knew Fred, you knew about the Jewish Home. Many individuals contribute to the Home today because of Fred. Others volunteer or serve on the Board because of him.

"There is no question about it, Fred Kravetz is the most important person I worked with, bar none. He was not the most polished guy, but certainly the most effective—he got things done. He was the best person to work with. He never said no when it came to the Home. In his own rough, tough way—which I loved—he was very supportive and generous. Fred's contributions of time, money and sheer will have given new meaning to the phrase Leadership by Example."

Past presidents of the Ladies Auxiliary at the 75th anniversary cele-bration. Seated in front, left to right, are Nathalie Goldberg, Phyllis Davidson, and Florence Rubens. Standing are Pearl Braiman, Shirley Axelrod, Helen Gordon, Florence Phillips, Margy Taylor, Ruth Shechet, Ethel Kowal, Enid Wallack, Essie Germanow, and Pinny Cooke.

1994 continued

Hundreds of people enjoy Grand Day, the Home's program for grandparents, children, and grandchildren. The program encourages visits and membership in the Golden Alliance.

The New York Association of Homes and Services for the Aging (NYAHSA) continues to push for reforms in New York State regulations concerning nursing homes, especially Medicaid funding. According to a NYAHSA report, "The real problem in New York is finding equitable financing which will lead to a customer-driven system."

The Eva and Benjamin Lipson Walkway is dedicated.

The Home undergoes corporate restructuring to "allow the Home to develop new services, and support programs for individuals living in their own homes."

Estelle B. Goldman donates a gift in honor of her late husband, M. Harry Goldman, to fund a garden.

Arnold S. Gissin receives the Lawrence A. Larson Award from the New York Association of Homes and Services for the Aging for his outstanding contribution to the care of the elderly in New York State.

The Home's total quality management program leads to numerous improvements.

The second Silver Salon opens. It is named in honor of the Myron S. Silver family, treasurer of the Jewish Home Foundation's Board of Directors, and a member of the Home's Board of Governors, who donated the salon's equipment.

DayTimers adds Early Bird Service, providing transportation to the adult day health center, breakfast, and help with hygiene and dressing.

Margy Taylor, and Pinny
Helen Gordon, Cooke.

Four generations
of the family of
Rae Smith.

Auxiliary hat fashion show, 1991.

Computerization of the long-term care industry's clinical and administrative effort soars in the early 1990s. The Home upgrades much of its equipment and software.

Norman and Burton Cohen give a generous gift to the Home in memory of their parents Abe and Esther Cohen, for the purchase of multi-media materials on Jewish culture, to be housed in the Natapow Library.

1995

The Home changes to a voice mail system to help manage its more than 600 calls a day.

The Department of Health once again finds no deficiencies at the Home during its survey.

The Home celebrates its 75th anniversary and begins using the phrase "A Family Among Families" to explain its mission.

The Home honors Elizabeth Schwartz, a long-time volunteer, on her 90th birthday.

Governor George Pataki's proposed funding cuts inspire a letter-writing campaign at the Home. The Home faces losing millions of dollars of Medicaid support and the end of DayTimers adult day care.

Major gifts include: the Adelaide and Robert Weinberg Fund, used for resident programming; the Minnie Cohen Fund, given by Erwin Atkins and Lillian Atkins, providing monthly Sunday entertainment for residents; the remodeling of Café Shalom, made possible with funds from the Brodsky family; and special audiovisual equipment purchased by the Wolk Foundation.

Jewish Home Auxiliary

The Auxiliary's phenomenally successful cookbook, put together by Annette Shapiro, Lois Mae E. Kuh, Miriam Wolff, Helen Gordon, Bea Rosenbloom, and a cast of hundreds.

I Remember

Helen Gordon reflects on her years of involvement with the Home.

"I first got active with Auxiliary in the late 1970s. I grew to appreciate the people there. I grew to know the residents and what they had to offer and grew to love them and learn from them. During my tenure as president, we worked on the project of producing little framed biographies of the residents. This allowed the staff to learn about them and gave stature to the residents and offered lines of communication.

"I think my major objective in everything I do for the Home is to help maintain a *heimish* atmosphere about the place. Auxiliary has tried very hard to achieve that. We must recall that the residents have identities, individualities and histories. The Café helps provide that sense of home— it is their kitchen.

"Two residents stand out in my mind. I ran a reminiscing group for a time. One woman was absolutely fantastic. I remember her telling a story of when your clothes go out of style you put them in a barrel and then after the barrel is full you turn it over and the clothes on the bottom are now in style again.

"Then there was a little lady who was not Jewish but who was there by choice. She used to call this 'my Jewish home' and she loved it.

"The Home is not perfect, but it is a wonderful setting for people who cannot live on their own. I think it gives them safety, companionship, comradeship, and a sense of identity. We are fortunate there is such a place."

The Summit at Brighton under construction.

Life Care Soars at The Summit at Brighton

It is clear that the Jewish Home of Rochester excels in providing high-quality care for the elderly. This is an expanding population. In 1980, there were 25.6 million Americans 65 and older; in 2030, there will be around 70 million. The needs of the elderly, however, are becoming more diverse as more and more people are able to lead vibrant lives well into their eighties, nineties and beyond. These vibrant seniors do, however, have other requirements that distinguish them from younger people. They need friends who are nearby, activities designed for their energy level, the comfort of having medical help easily accessible, and people who will assist with transportation, shopping and meals.

As early as the mid-1960s, the Board recognized the need for such a facility. Discussions, site locations, surveys, and fund-raising were a periodic topic of conversation and planning for the Board. However, until the monumental task of building and financing the new structure on South Winton Road could be accomplished, the discussions remained theoretical. In the fall of 1985, board members began again in earnest, led by Mike Silver, an early advocate of the concept, his brother-in-law Burt Tanenbaum, Fred Kravetz and later Julian Gordon. The Jewish Home Foundation and its leaders were extremely influential in this endeavor as well. They all demonstrated the kind of strategic thinking, foresight, commitment and courage that has characterized the leader-

ship of the Home for nearly eighty years.

To serve the needs of a growing population of well older people who deserve the benefits of companionship, kosher food, proper care, recreation, social atmosphere and a Jewish ambiance in a life care facility, the Home is now completing an elaborate retirement community on a separate, spacious 25-acre site on an adjacent campus. Designed by Boston architect Peter I. Shaffer, The Summit is the first life care community in western New York and only the third such community authorized by New York State. Life Care allows Summit members to transfer to assisted living or nursing home care at the same monthly maintenance fee as living in their apartment. The threat of losing one's life savings for

nursing care is thereby eliminated.

The Summit at Brighton offers 93 one- or two-bedroom independent apartments as well as 30 enriched-living suites for people who need additional care. Summit members pay a 90 percent refundable entrance fee and a monthly maintenance fee for upkeep, meals, rent and services. Members receive handsome apartments with specially designed features that cater to older people, such as special outlets, railings and emergency response systems. Critical to the Summit lifestyle is an expansive commons area with dining facilities, library, recreational rooms, health facilities, swimming pool, outdoor ponds, tennis court, putting green and walking trails. Members also have access to housekeepers, transportation to and from local events and stores, one daily meal (lunch or dinner) served in a restaurant-type setting

and a full program of outings to theaters and films, as well as social activities on the premises. If a member ever needs enriched living or nursing home care, that care is provided for as long as it is needed at no additional cost—the life care component.

"It's as attractive as any resort one might go to," comments Arnold Gissin. "It offers the most flexible living arrangements, comprehensive care as needed, and the first and only guaranteed financial security arrangement for retirees in our area. And it all takes place in a beautiful new community designed for the active, independent lifestyles of healthy older adults. As one's needs increase, one's costs remain the same."

"Continuing care retirement communities are a preferred mode of living for retirees all over the country, but we believe we are creating something even more valuable, with guaranteed health care to the people who live at

The Summit. This is an opportunity for the entire Rochester community," noted Julian Gordon, co-chair of The Summit Steering Committee.

"The Summit offers an enhanced retirement lifestyle," he continued. "It provides the opportunity to spend an active, independent retirement among friends, near family, and to remain a vital part of the community. At the same time, Rochester's Jewish community is enriched by our connections with our parents and grandparents, the people who are the foundations of our families. They strengthen our community, and ultimately we all benefit." Many of the first residents of The Summit have ties to the Jewish Home stretching back to the 1920s and 1930s.

The Auxiliary has 1,000 members, 292 of whom are life members.

The Home is chosen as a Best Practices recipient for its Russian language program. Arnold Gissin reports to the Board that "Soviet immigrants are hired by the Home through Jewish Family Service, which has proven to be a very successful relationship. The Foundation of the Jewish Community Federation provided the Home with grant money, which has enabled JHR to offer bilingual classes."

1996

Cutbacks in New York State funding are not as severe as expected, and the DayTimers program continues.

New Horizons expands its services and hours of operation to three days a week.

David G. Ross, attorney and partner, Ross & Gould-Ross, was named chairman of the Jewish Home of Rochester Board of Directors.

An Information Center opens at 95 Allens Creek Road for The Summit.

Major refurbishing brightens the Home's main lobby and cafeteria.

A new porch/solarium opens at the Home's North entrance at the end of the Street of Shops. The solarium was made possible by the generosity of Eli and Mildred Sokol, who presented their gift to the Home Foundation at its 75th anniversary.

Artist Jack Wolsky joins Sue Klein and Etta Atkin in teaching art to residents.

The Auxiliary publishes *Beyond Chicken Soup*, which includes thousands of recipes drawn from the Jewish community. The book brings $40,000 profit to the Home and goes into a second printing.

From Winton Road to The Summit

Reflections

The Jewish Home has faced many challenges since it moved to the new facility in 1985—financial, political, sociological. People are living longer, individuals are coming to the Home older and sicker, many suffering from dementia requiring intensive and expensive care. Perhaps no challenge is more basic, however, than its desire to preserve the commitment to caring that was its hallmark from its earliest days on St. Paul Street and yet find a way to keep the level of efficiency and technological and medical innovation high. The world is changing and the Home has changed with it, often taking the lead. That certainly is exemplified by its magnificent new facility, the opening of The Summit at Brighton as a new concept for services for the elderly, initiatives it has taken in adult day services, the restraint-free environment, and involvement with geriatric education and research in areas such as geriatric pain.

Dr. Bernard Shore is recognized as one of the outstanding medical directors in the country. Arnold Gissin has put together a dedicated and excellent staff, shaped by his qualities of leadership, innovation, professionalism and caring. "He is an 'action' person and is not opposed to change," Joel Kellmanson remarked. That spirit permeates the staff. "We've always been 'culture-changers.' We've always been pioneers," remarked Gissin. But to the credit of the Board of Directors and Governors, all of these changes have taken place within a Jewish context of caring and responsibility.

The Board has held true to its mission even when it has been expensive to do so. Through the Depression of the 1930s, the recession of the 1980s and the reimbursement cutbacks of the 1990s, the Home stayed committed to its mission of providing the highest quality of care in a Jewish environment. That was its reason for being in 1920, and it remains true today. It has been blessed with able leaders and hundreds of dedicated volunteers—people like Irving Ring, Evalyn Phillips and Aaron Braveman, to name just three, who have given so generously of their time and worked directly with the residents of the Home. A new generation of younger activists, individuals like Joel Kellmanson (president, 1994-96) and David Ross (president, 1996-98), have accepted the mantle of leadership and have made important contributions. Reorganization of the bylaws and corporate structure of the Home was accomplished in 1994-95, leading to the creation of a parent corporation called Jewish Health Care Systems, with James Littwitz its first chairperson. This gives the Home more flexibility in this rapidly changing health care environment.

The Jewish Home of Rochester stands poised to take its solid legacy into the next century. There will be challenges and transformations—there always are—but as long as it remains true to its past and retains the institu-

The Auxiliary invites Jewish residents from area nursing homes to come to the Jewish Home for seders.

The Home collaborates with St. Ann's, St. John's, The Friendly Home, and the Episcopal Church Home to find creative solutions for common challenges, including the development of long-term care insurance.

For the fifth year, the Department of Health announces a deficiency-free survey for the Home.

A dementia unit accommodating 38 residents opens on the sixth floor.

The Louis S. and Molly B. Wolk Foundation makes a gift to purchase much-needed equipment for Home residents, including an EKG machine, wheelchairs, motorized low beds, over-the-bed tables, and physical therapy equipment.

The Home helps establish the Senior Health Alliance of Greater Rochester.

1997
Residents take advantage of instruction in Tai Chi, a martial art form.

The Home offers Traditions in Caring home care in conjunction with four other senior health providers, St. Anne's Home, St. John's Home, the Episcopal Church Home, and the Friendly Home.

Kosher Meals-On-Wheels becomes available. The Home partners with the Visiting Nurse Service to offer this program.

The Golden Alliance has 530 members.

1998
The Summit opens, ushering in a new chapter in services for the elderly.

---

tional flexibility and courage that come with experience and confidence in a job well done and the vigor and energy that derive from its dedicated lay supporters and professionals, it will remain Rochester's "family among families."

It may seem like a long way from St. Paul Street, but the Home has always been about people—the tens of thousands of people it has cared for with skill, warmth and dignity, and the thousands of dedicated leaders and volunteers who have made the Home the pillar in the Jewish community it has become. As David Ross expressed it: "There is still the underlying basic commitment to care for the Jewish elderly. No matter how the emphasis changes, no matter how the funding stream changes, or how the regulatory pattern changes, that is still the job that has to be done." The Home's family of supporters internalized instinctively that ancient Jewish teaching from Proverbs: "Teach us to count our days so that we will acquire a heart of wisdom."

Residents enjoying a nice spring day.

127

OFFICERS OF THE JEWISH HOME 1920 TO 1997

1920s

Sam Ball
Irving Bieber
William Brown
William Feinbloom
David Goldman
Mrs. T. Goldman
Mrs. R. Goldstein
Isaac Hershberg
Max L. Holtz

Sol Levin
Solomon Levin
David Neimkin
* Lester Nusbaum
Morris Rosenbloom
Frank Sherman
Joseph E. Silverstein
Anna Wolfe

1930s

Samuel Ball
Samuel Bloom
William Brown
Allen Eber
Maurice G. Ellenbogen
Sigmund Firestone
Sidney Grossman

Max L. Holtz
Mrs. A. F. Horowitz
Dr. J. S. Kominz
Solomon Levin
David Neimkin
* Lester Nusbaum
Morris Rosenbloom

1940s

Samuel Ball
Samuel Bloom
Abraham Cherkass
Allen Eber
Harry Z. Harris
Ben Leve

Solomon Levin
* Garson Meyer
* Lester Nusbaum
Abraham Plaksin
Joseph E. Silverstein

1950s

* Jacob Ark
Samuel Ball
Samuel Bloom
* Ruben Dankoff
Allen Eber
Harry Germanow
Harry Goldman
* Samuel H. Greenhouse
Harry Harris
David Lazeroff

Eli Leven
* Garson Meyer
Lester Nusbaum
Benjamin Robfogel
Jack Rubens
Dr. Morris Shapiro
Harold Siegel
Joseph Silverstein
Leon Sturman

1960s

Allen Eber
* Leon Germanow
Emanuel Goldberg
Irving Kessler
* Eli Leven
* Morton Nusbaum

Samuel Poze
Herman Schwartz
Dr. Morris Shapiro
Harold Siegel
Joseph Silverstein
Casper Solomon

1970s

Peter Adelstein
* Donald Cohn
Allen Eber
David Eisenberg
Dr. William Feldman
* Emanuel Goldberg
Irving L. Kessler
James K. Littwitz

Herbert F. Mock
James L. Robfogel
Herman H. Schwartz
Dr. Morris Shapiro
Irwin S. Shulman
* Myron Silver
Casper Solomon
Burton Tanenbaum

1980s

Martin Bael
Dr. Herbert S. Elins
Henry P. Epstein
David Gordon
Orry Jacobs
* Ethel Kowal
Robert S. Landsman
James K. Littwitz
* Dr. Martin Nacman
Betty Oppenheimer

Melvyn J. Poplock
Dr. Donna Regenstreif
James L. Robfogel
* Ruth B. Rosenberg
Dr. Morris J. Shapiro
Dr. Ben Sischy
Peter G. Smith
* Burton D. Tanenbaum
Dr. Harold Tragash

1990s

Howard Berman
Stuart Bobry
Ellen Croog
David Gordon
* Julian Gordon
* Joel Kellmanson
Ethel A. Kowal

Fred B. Kravetz
James K. Littwitz
Melvyn J. Poplock
* David Ross
* Dr. Morris J. Shapiro
James B. Silverman
Morris Weinstein

* President

A TRADITION OF LEADERSHIP

Great institutions like the Jewish Home do not thrive without great leadership. One of the Jewish Home's proudest traditions is the visionary leadership of its Board members and the presidents under which they served. We are privileged to acknowledge the Home's past presidents, along with a partial list of their accomplishments.

Lester Nusbaum
1920-1942
The first president of the Home. His vision established the standard of excellence that distinguishes the Home to this day.

Garson Meyer
1943-1952
An integral part of the planning and development of the Home's first modern five-story brick and steel structure.

Ruben A. Dankoff
1953-1955
A moving force in the creation and realization of the new Home and the 60-bed infirmary wing addition.

Samuel H. Greenhouse
1956-1958
Created an adult education program for residents and explored the extension of the Home's programs and services to non-residents.

Justice Jacob Ark
1958-1961
Established the dental and eye clinics, the podiatry and laboratory services. Inaugurated the "semi-infirmary" third level of care, a pioneering innovation.

Eli A. Leven, M.D.
1962-1964
Oversaw the Home's increasing emergence as a rehabilitation center.

Morton Nusbaum
1965-1967
Completed a major renovation and modernization of the 1950-54 facility.

Leon M. Germanow
1968-1970
Opened the new 60-bed medical wing and Activity Center.

Emanuel Goldberg
1971-1973
Began planning for future projects, including housing and day care. Raised $900,000 for new medical wing and Activity Center.

Myron S. Silver
1974-1976
Inaugurated New Horizons, the senior adult day care program. Began efforts to secure a campus complex site. Was co-chair of the New Building Fund Campaign.

Donald M. Cohn
1977-1979
Worked with deep commitment on the campus complex project. Developed the Family Council for the Home's residents.

Ruth B. Rosenberg
1980-1983
Was instrumental in the planning for the new facility at Winton Road South.

Martin Nacman, D.S.W.
1983-1985
Oversaw the move to the new facility and promoted the Home as a geriatric teaching center.

Burton D. Tanenbaum
1986-1988
The Home's first president at the new facility. Initiated a study on corporate restructuring; began a funding relationship with the Jewish Community Federation.

Ethel A. Kowal
1988-1990
Assisted president and chief executive officer Arnold Gissin in the implementation of the Home's pioneering restraint-free program.

Morris J. Shapiro, M.D.
1990-1992
Set the stage for the settlement of a long-standing reimbursement dispute with New York State; drew local Jewish agencies together in a spirit of cooperation and support; co-chair of the Building Fund Campaign.

Julian M. Gordon
1992-1994
One of the prime voices in the development of the Senior Living Project. The Home's reimbursement dispute with the state was also resolved during his presidency.

Joel Kellmanson
1994-1996
Oversaw the dedication of the Atkin Center and the expansion of the Home's adult day programs. He continued the development of the Senior Living Project, including the purchase of the property on which it is being constructed.

David Ross
1996-1998
Worked to implement the corporate reorganization and oversee planning for the future, including the collaboration with other health care providers and other Jewish agencies.

A u x i l i a r y   P r e s i d e n t s

Hattie Neisner	1933-1940
Sarah Levinson	1940-1949
Florence Rubens	1949-1951
Phyllis Davidson	1951-1953
Essie Germanow	1953-1955
Vi Rosenthal	1955-1957
Pinny Cooke	1957-1959
Ginni Nusbaum	1959-1961
Rose Wolfe	1961-1963
Nathalie Goldberg	1963-1965
Beatrice Goran	1965-1967
Ethel Kowal	1967-1969
Min Edelman	1969-1979
Shirley Axelrod	1971-1973
Elizabeth Rudman	1973-1975
Pearl Braiman	1975-1977
Helen Silver	1977-1979
Enid Wallack	1979-1981
Harriet Lewis	1981-1983
Ruth Shechet	1983-1985
Mildred Schirer	1985-1987
Florence Phillips	1987-1989
Margy Taylor	1989-1991
Helen Gordon	1991-1993
Donna Cohen	1993-1995
Ruth Shechet	1995-1996
Naomi Friedman	1997-1998

JEWISH HOME FOUNDATION OFFICERS

1979-1980
(First Board)
Hyman Friedman, *President*
Sherman Levey, *Vice President*
Helen K. Silver, *Secretary*
Sidney Peck, *Treasurer*

1981, 1982, 1983
Sherman Levey, *President*
Donald M. Cohn, *Vice President*
Helen K. Silver, *Secretary*
Sidney Peck, *Treasurer*

1984, 1985, 1986
Donald M. Cohn, *President*
John E. Lovenheim,
   Vice President
Helen K. Silver, *Secretary*
Sidney Peck, *Treasurer*

1986
John E. Lovenheim, *President*
Edward D. Bloom, *Vice President*
Helen K. Silver, *Secretary*
Sidney Peck, *Treasurer*

1987
John E. Lovenheim, *President*
Edward D. Bloom, *Vice President*
Burton D. Tanenbaum, *Secretary*
Sidney Peck, *Treasurer*

1988
Myron S. Silver, *President*
Edward D. Bloom, *Vice President*
Burton Tanenbaum, *Secretary*
Sidney Peck, *Treasurer*

1989
Myron S. Silver, *President*
Edward D. Bloom, *Vice President*
Burton Tanenbaum, *Secretary*
Fred B. Kravetz, *Treasurer*

1990
Myron S. Silver, *President*
Edward D. Bloom, *Vice President*
Burton Tanenbaum, *Secretary*
Fred B. Kravetz, *Treasurer*

1991
Edward D. Bloom, *President*
Elaine G. Kellmanson,
   Vice President
John E. Lovenheim, *Secretary*
Fred B. Kravetz, *Treasurer*

1992
Edward Bloom, *President*
Elaine G. Kellmanson,
   Vice President
John E. Lovenheim, *Secretary*
Fred B. Kravetz, *Treasurer*

1993
Edward Bloom, *President*
Elaine G. Kellmanson,
   Vice President
John E. Lovenheim, *Secretary*
Fred B. Kravetz, *Treasurer*

1994
Edward Bloom, *President*
Elaine G. Kellmanson,
   Vice President
John E. Lovenheim, *Secretary*
Fred B. Kravetz, *Treasurer*

1995
Edward Bloom, *President*
Elaine G. Kellmanson,
   Vice President
John E. Lovenheim, *Secretary*
Myron S. Silver, *Treasurer*

1996
Edward Bloom, *President*
Elaine G. Kellmanson,
   Vice President
John E. Lovenheim, *Secretary*
Myron S. Silver, *Treasurer*

1997
Edward Bloom, *President*
Elaine G. Kellmanson,
   Vice President
John E. Lovenheim, *Secretary*
Myron S. Silver, *Treasurer*

Thank you

*The Jewish Home
Foundation wishes
to recognize and
thank the following
for their part
in producing
this book:*

Adelaide Weinberg
Robert Weinberg
Michael Dobkowski
Marcia Falk
Lynne Feldman
Arnold Gissin
Ceil Goldman
Alan M. Greenberg
Will Greenberg
Barbara Kuter
Anna Lanzatella
Barbara I. Lovenheim
John Lovenheim
Kathleen M. Mannix
Lawrence Milstein
Louise Novros
Rochester Public Library
Linda Rubens
Eli Rudin
Catherine R. Samson
Elizabeth Schwartz
The Stinehour Press
Don Strand Photography
The Strong Museum

The Archives Committee
William Greenberg
Co-chairperson
Judy Lurie
Co-chairperson

Myron Bernhardt
Aaron Braveman
David Eisenberg
Helen Gordon
Sue Klein
John Lovenheim
Eli Rudin
Elizabeth Schwartz

BLESS OUR HOME
"O Lord I Pray..."

Steel, bricks and mortar could never make a home,
Travel the world over wherever you may roam.
It takes a wealth of family and tenderness of the heart,
Where care, love, and compassion never would depart.

In our Rochester community, such an establishment began.
Some seventy-five years later, it resides on rich fertile land.
And here, a resident of need, wherein each golden year,
Finds a place within a family without a necessity to fear.

May success engulf it always, as days slip quickly by,
And our Maker forthwith bless it, from a position in the sky.
Take care future generations of the story written in this book,
About a miracle derived by the determined courage that it took.

Sailing forth through gusty seas, the Home may need a port.
Then, this younger generation will have a ball within their court.
It could take the wisdom of Solomon with lessons from the past,
For into these guiding hands, our Home's destiny is cast.

Upon strong shoulders perpetual achievements has become our goal,
Carrying forth superb accomplishments recorded now from such worthy toil.
And toil it will be by many experts throughout the years,
By applying rare skills, when needed, with their blood, sweat and tears.

. . . and make it safe both night and day.

Bob Weinberg